Second Edition

Skillful 2

Reading & Writing Student's Book

Author: Louis Rogers
Series Consultant: Dorothy E. Zen

D1438553

macmillan
education

Grammar	Writing	Study skills	Unit outcomes
Use discourse markers of contrast and comparison	Write paragraphs that give balanced opinions Brainstorm, plan, and write a paragraph explaining and justifying your opinion about how polite young people are today	Start a reflective learning journal to help you assess your progress	Read topic sentences to understand the main ideas in texts Read texts to identify arguments and opinions Compose and edit a paragraph using discourse markers of contrast and techniques for writing balanced opinions
Use relative clauses	Write compound sentences to express more complex ideas Plan, write, and edit a paragraph describing food production in your country	Learn tricks to help you start writing	Practice summarizing main ideas in texts Use synonyms to identify repeated ideas and main topics Compose and edit a paragraph using relative clauses and compound sentences
Use modals of obligation and necessity	Practice writing essay introductions Prepare, write, and edit an introduction to an essay on the importance of customer service in business	Identify the soft skills that recruiters are looking for	Read texts to identify supporting information Use signposting to identify main ideas and text organization Brainstorm and compose an essay introduction using modals of obligation and necessity
Use irregular verbs in the simple past	Practice summarizing trends in graphs Brainstorm, plan, and write a summary of trends in a graph	Use headings, labels, and keys to help you understand data in tables, charts, and graphs	Read texts to understand different kinds of data Read texts to identify primary and secondary research Prepare and edit a summary of trends in a graph
Use determiners of quantity	Practice describing locations and changes on maps and diagrams Brainstorm, plan, and write a description of changes and improvements to an area of farmland shown on two plans	Think about your vision of success as a student	Practice identifying pronoun reference Read texts to identify reasons that explain or support main ideas Prepare and edit a description of changes shown on two plans

6 PRESSURE **PAGE 98** **Culture** ➤ **Article:** Pressure on parents **Sociology** ➤ **Magazine article:** Rich and famous	Stress relief therapy	Practice identifying cause and effect relationships Identify tone in an article to help you understand the author's opinion	Practice and use phrases for hedging and boosting
7 FEAR **PAGE 116** **Sociology** ➤ **Magazine article:** Fears, learning, coping **Biology** ➤ **Article:** Fight or flight	Arachnophobia	Practice deducing the meaning of new words from context Practice identifying definitions in texts	Practice and use verb and preposition collocations
8 STORIES **PAGE 134** **History** ➤ **Biographical article:** National hero **Culture** ➤ **Article:** The power of the written word	An adventurer returns	Practice distinguishing between facts and assumptions Identify bridge sentences to better understand text organization	Practice and use adverbs and adverbial phrases of time
9 ENVIRONMENT **PAGE 152** **Conservation** ➤ **Essay:** Rainforests of the sea **Wildlife protection** ➤ **Essay:** Living together	Coming home to nest	Scan texts for examples that support the main idea Scan texts for examples listed in groups of three	Practice and use words to describe environmental issues
10 MEDICINE **PAGE 170** **Med tech** ➤ **Magazine article:** Self-diagnosis **Health** ➤ **Essay:** A good night's sleep	Smart eye exams	Practice taking notes in your own words when reading Form research questions to focus your reading	Practice and use words to describe medical symptoms

Use present conditionals	Practice writing paragraphs on causes and effects Plan, write, and edit two cause and effect paragraphs on the effects of pressure on children today	Identify triggers to help you deal with stress	Read texts to identify cause and effect Practice identifying tone Brainstorm and compose two cause and effect paragraphs
Use present perfect simple	Practice organizing your notes into essay paragraphs Compose, share, and edit two paragraphs about the pros and cons of fear	Practice giving and receiving feedback and criticism	Read texts to deduce meaning of new words from context Practice identifying definitions in texts Compose and edit two pros and cons paragraphs about fear
Use past perfect and simple past	Practice using topic sentences, bridge sentences, and concluding sentences to improve essay structure Plan, write, and share two paragraphs on the story of an important invention or discovery	Improve your core research skills by narrowing your search criteria	Read to distinguish between facts and assumptions Practice identifying bridge sentences Write and edit two narrative paragraphs about an invention or discovery
Use present and past perfect passives	Practice summarizing arguments in an essay conclusion Brainstorm, compose, and revise a conclusion to an essay about an environmental issue in your country	Identify strategies to solve problems creatively	Practice scanning for examples Practice scanning for examples listed in groups Plan and compose an essay conclusion about an environmental issue
Use reported speech	Practice proofreading and editing your writing Plan, write, and edit an opinion essay on the merits of self-diagnosis	Think critically when writing	Practice note-taking when reading Form research questions to inform how you read Write and edit an opinion essay about self-diagnosis

To the student

Academic success requires so much more than memorizing facts. It takes skills. This means that a successful student can both learn and think critically.

Skillful gives you:

- Skills you need to succeed when reading and listening to academic texts
- Skills you need to succeed when writing for and speaking to different audiences
- Skills for critically examining the issues presented by a speaker or a writer
- Study skills for learning and remembering the English language and important information.

To successfully use this book, use these strategies:

Come to class prepared to learn. This means that you should show up well fed, well rested, and prepared with the proper materials. Watch the video online and look at the discussion point before starting each new unit.

Ask questions and interact. Learning a language is not passive. You need to actively participate. Help your classmates, and let them help you. It is easier to learn a language with other people.

Practice! Memorize and use new language. Use the *Skillful* online practice to develop the skills presented in the Student's Book. Revise vocabulary on the review page.

Review your work. Look over the skills, grammar, and vocabulary from previous units. Study a little bit each day, not just before tests.

Be an independent learner, too. Look for opportunities to study and practice English outside of class, such as reading for pleasure and using the Internet in English. Remember that learning skills, like learning a language, takes time and practice. Be patient with yourself, but do not forget to set goals.

I hope you enjoy using *Skillful*! Check your progress and be proud of your success!

Dorothy E. Zemach – Series Consultant

Opening page

Each unit starts with two opening pages. These pages get you ready to study the topic of the unit. There is a video to watch and activities to do before you start your class.

Reading lessons

In every unit, there are two reading lessons and they present two different aspects of the unit topic and help you with ideas and language for your writing task.

Vocabulary to prepare you for the reading activities

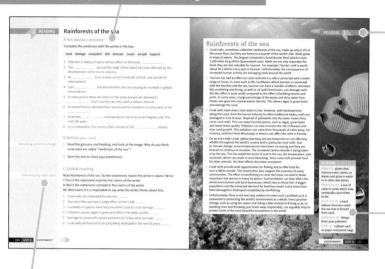

Every reading section helps you use a new reading skill.

Glossaries help you understand higher level words from the reading text.

Develop your reading skills in each part of the reading lesson.

Writing lessons

After your reading lessons, there is a page for you to analyze a model answer to a writing task. This will help you organize your ideas and language and prepare for your final task at the end of the unit.

First, analyze the model answer.

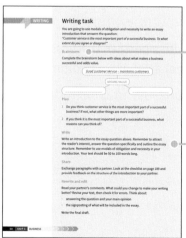

Brainstorm and plan your final writing task.

Finally, write your paragraph or essay.

Next, discuss your ideas.

Discussion point

Discuss with a partner.

1 Is attitude to time in your country more like Brazil or Australia?

The attitude in my country is …

2 What advice would you give someone about meals in your country?

During meals it's important to …

3 What is a polite way to greet someone in your country? What other greetings do you know from around the world?

Men and women greet each other by …

GLOBAL POLITENESS

Australia
Arriving on time to meet people is very important.

Brazil
It is OK to be a little late.

Greece
Shake hands when you meet people and to say goodbye.

Morocco
It is polite to offer fresh mint tea to visitors.

Poland
Bread and salt are used to welcome important guests.

Japan
You should remove your shoes when you enter someone's home.

U.K.
Sometimes people don't make eye contact during a conversation.

VIDEO

TABLE MANNERS

Before you watch

Work with a partner. Discuss the following situations. Are there any rules about polite behavior in your culture?

1 Putting your arms on the table at dinner.
2 Bringing a present for your host.
3 The way you eat your food.

UNIT AIMS

READING 1 Using topic sentences to understand main ideas
READING 2 Identifying arguments and opinions
STUDY SKILL Reflective learning journals

VOCABULARY Giving your opinion
GRAMMAR Discourse markers of contrast and comparison
WRITING Writing a balanced opinion

Traditional Japanese business greeting.

While you watch

Read the questions and then watch the video. Circle the correct answers.

1 The students are attending classes in
   a manners.
   b international business.

2 Which one of these is not a rule of the classes?
   a To not put your elbows on the table
   b To move the chair for a guest

3 The cost of the classes is
   a $75 an hour.
   b $75 for 16 weeks.

After you watch

Answer the questions with a partner.

1 Do you think it's important to learn about other cultures?

   Yes, because …

2 What things are different in your culture to other cultures?

   In my culture we …

3 Imagine you work for an international company. Would you pay for a course to learn about other cultures?

What does *polite* mean to you?

A Vocabulary preview

1 Complete the sentences with the words in the box.

behavior	consider	judge	manners	rude	smiling	social media	tip

1 Some people think it is _____ to speak loudly on your phone in public.

2 _____ has changed the way people communicate. Some people think connecting online has made people less polite.

3 Our _____, the way we act, affects people's opinions of us.

4 It is good _____ to hold a door open for someone.

5 We _____ people by how they act as much as by what they say.

6 _____ is a helpful way to show we are friendly, or to make others feel relaxed.

7 It is important to _____ when the service is good.

8 We don't all _____ politeness to be important.

2 Check (✓) the sentences you agree with. Compare your opinions with a partner.

B Before you read

Preparing to read

1 Look at these behaviors. Choose how acceptable the behavior is.

	Very rude					It's fine
Speaking on your phone on public transportation	10	8	6	4	2	1
Interrupting someone	10	8	6	4	2	1
Using your left hand to greet someone	10	8	6	4	2	1
Sending e-mails during a meeting	10	8	6	4	2	1

2 Compare your choices with a partner. Give reasons for your choice.

What does *polite* mean to you?

1 In many countries around the world, no matter what generation you are, there are some key things that are considered polite behavior. Turning your phone off at dinner, turning it down on public transportation, not interrupting colleagues, saying please and thank you, and offering seats to those less able to stand than you are all considered appropriate and polite behavior in many cultures. Although most people agree these behaviors are polite, there is a big difference in politeness between the generations. It was once considered polite to stand when someone left the dinner table, but this is no longer the case. Additionally, older generations are the most likely to judge someone's politeness, but what other factors influence politeness in society?

2 While languages change over time in terms of words being added or taken away, they also change in terms of their structure and use. Some phrases are not really used for their actual meaning but as polite social phrases. For example, when someone says "thank you," how should we reply? Older people are more likely to say "You're welcome," whereas younger people are more likely to say "No problem." The concepts of polite behavior don't just vary by age, they also vary by geographic location. How we display polite behavior in one place is quite different in another.

3 From tipping, to smiling, and how you eat, there are different ways to show politeness across the world. Take tipping for instance, which is polite and expected in countries such as the U.S.A. However, in Japan tipping is not expected in any situation and may even create a difficult situation by offending someone. The hand you use to do different things is not important in most European cultures, but in India the left hand is considered unclean and shouldn't be used to eat, greet, or exchange money. Some people now even argue that asking for directions is rude. People have phones for that and should not need to interrupt other people.

4 This is not the only influence technology is having on what is considered polite behavior. Cell phones have changed what is considered polite behavior in many situations. To some people even just having your phone at the dinner table is thought to be impolite. An even greater number are likely to consider speaking on the phone during dinner as rude. However, some people argue that there are differences in this depending on people's age. Take sending e-mails in a meeting from your phone. Many younger people are likely to consider this as acceptable whereas older people are much more likely to have a negative reaction and find this rude. Overall those under 30 are arguably much more tolerant of people using cell devices at a meal, during a meeting, or in a class. Younger generations simply have a different perspective on what is socially acceptable behavior when it comes to using technology. Digital devices are not only changing how we behave but also what we consider polite behavior.

5 The concept of politeness varies greatly across cultures and generations. What is acceptable in one context may cause great offence in another. Adapting our behavior to suit other people and the situation is a skill we all need to learn.

GLOSSARY

offend (v) to make someone upset and angry by doing or saying something

Using topic sentences to understand main ideas

C Global reading

> Topic sentences are usually one of the first two sentences of each paragraph. They contain the main idea of the paragraph and everything in that paragraph should support the main idea. Reading topic sentences is a good way to scan a text quickly.

1 Read *What does polite mean to you?* and underline the topic sentences in paragraphs 2–4.

2 Match the main ideas below with paragraphs 2–4.

A People use different phrases for politeness. ___

B Technology has changed what is thought of as polite. ___

C Politeness varies across cultures. ___

D Close reading

Scanning

Read *What does polite mean to you?* again and complete the paragraph.

The attitudes to polite behavior change depending on age, but also on geography. For example, in response to "thank you," older people are likely to say [1]_____ and younger generations would say [2]_____. In other countries, customs change too: [3]_____ is not common in Japan, and in India you shouldn't use your [4]_____ for eating or greeting. Recently, technology has also changed our polite behavior norms. A few people think [5]_____ with you while you eat is rude, and [6]_____ often do not think it's OK to send e-mails during a meeting.

E Critical thinking

1 What behavior do you find rude in other people? Do you think other people would find any of your behavior rude?

I really dislike it when …

2 Do you think younger people are less polite than older people? Why / why not?

I do / don't think so because …

Study skills Reflective learning journals

In a strong notebook, or using your computer, start a reflective learning journal.

Why?

Writing things down helps you to clarify your thoughts and emotions, to work out strategies, and to focus on your development and progress. A written record will help you see how you are progressing from week to week, and from semester to semester.

Who is it for?

For yourself—to help you focus on your own development.

© Stella Cottrell (2013)

1 Look at these academic and language learning challenges. Put them on the line to rank them from easiest to most difficult.

(a) academic reading   (b) essay writing   (c) giving presentations
(d) learning new vocabulary   (e) researching for essays
(f) revision for tests   (g) time management

easy   difficult

2 Compare your line with a partner. How do you deal with the most difficult tasks?

3 Read about *Reflective learning journals.* How could a reflective learning journal help with two of the problems in Exercise 1?

_____

_____

4 Read the questions below. Select the ones you think you would find most interesting to write about in a journal. Compare your choices with a partner.

1 How do you feel about your course?
   Excited, worried, determined

2 How can you assess your progress?
   Grades, teacher feedback, finding tasks easier

3 What things do you find difficult?
   Math, essays, presentations

4 How do you learn best?
   At home, in class, with friends, alone

Social media society

A Vocabulary preview

1 Match the words in bold with the correct definitions.

1 **anxious** (adj)	a extremely unkind, or causing someone to be unhappy or upset
2 **cruel** (adj)	b the writing or pictures on a computer screen that you can see at one time, for example as part of a website
3 **get attention** (phrase)	
4 **hurt** (v)	c to get someone's interest or to make someone notice something
5 **opinion** (n)	d worried because you think something bad might happen
6 **page** (n)	e a place on the Internet where information is available about a particular subject, organization, etc.
7 **post** (v)	
8 **site** (n)	f to cause someone pain or injury
	g to put writing or images online where other people can see them
	h the attitude that you have towards something, especially your thoughts about how good it is

2 Choose the correct word to complete the questions.

1 Which social media **sites / opinions** are most popular in your country?

2 How many times a day do you **get attention / post** something online?

3 Do you click on advertising on different web **pages / opinions**?

4 Do you worry your comments might **hurt / post** someone's feelings?

5 When you put things on social media do you care about other people's **pages / opinions**?

6 What do you do when someone writes something negative or **cruel / anxious** about someone you know?

7 Do you feel **cruel / anxious** when people do not reply to your messages?

8 Do you like it when one of your pictures or videos gets a lot of **attention / anxious** from other people?

3 Discuss the questions from Exercise 2 with a partner.

B Before you read

Predicting

Read the first sentence of *Social media society*. Work with a partner and predict the topics the text might cover.

SOCIAL MEDIA
SOCIETY

1 Social media is changing everything

Social media is changing how we communicate, how we do business, and how we live in society. People use it to stay in touch with others, to get people's attention and to check the news. People can connect with celebrities and even communicate with members of the government through their social media profile. When we consider this is only 20 or 30 years after the start of the Web it is not surprising that it is considered one of the biggest ever changes in modern society. So, has social media been a positive or negative development for society?

2 People are less connected

Many people argue that social media makes young people antisocial. In 1998 psychiatrist Tamaki Saito invented the term "hikikomori" which translates into English as avoiding social contact. It describes a growing number of young men who shut themselves away in their bedrooms from society and use technology more and more. Some people think there are between a quarter and one million people like this in Japan. Research around the world suggests this is not only a Japanese problem but one that exists around the world.

3 The only way to socialize

However, other people believe that social media is not more popular because young people are more antisocial. In comparison to the past, many children are not allowed out as much to play. As a result, many use social media to stay in touch with friends because they are not allowed to see them as often. Teenagers want to spend time together and social media is allowing them more contact than they could normally have. It also allows them to feel part of a wider group.

4 Not just for young people

Some think the Internet is just for young people, but this trend is slowly changing. One of the fastest growing groups of social media users is now grandparents who are using it to keep in touch with other people. Since people now move around a lot for work, many grandparents use it to keep in touch with their own children or grandchildren. It also provides the opportunity to socialize when people cannot move around as much as they once did. From reconnecting with old friends to adding new ones, social media has a big positive effect on how we communicate.

5 Online profile

Though social media helps us to communicate with other people, it can also change how we see ourselves. Some argue that social media makes us compare ourselves more to other people because we often just post the highlights of our lives. This makes us feel anxious about what other people think of us and can make people depressed. When we see the lives of celebrities and profiles of companies, many people forget that it is carefully created and not real. Both the companies and people use social media to create an image and a version of themselves. Like these people, even most normal people only show the interesting parts of their lives. Selfies are rarely the first photo someone took. People take hundreds until they get the right photo that gets the attention and comments they want.

6 Being popular

Equally, social media is now often considered a popularity contest. From how many people follow us to how many "likes" we get, it can have a big effect on how we feel about ourselves. People often feel anxious about how many "likes" they get on a picture or comment. Many people feel hurt if people don't like their pictures or posts. People are often so worried about displaying their life in a way that makes them look interesting that they spend less time actually doing healthy activities with other people. This is connected to our human need to feel part of a group. Unfortunately, many connections and friendships online are not real friendships. Of course, many people do have good friends online, but at the same time we can have many false connections just to make ourselves feel more popular.

7 Wanting everything now

Social media also makes us want everything now. The idea of wanting something immediately is connected to another basic human need for food, water, and shelter. However, this need means we now want the latest phone, tablet, or car straight away. Social media increases this feeling. We can upload videos, photos, and updates and get quick feedback from our network. We reply almost immediately to e-mails and posts. There are many instances where certain things in life are better. We no longer have to send letters and wait days or weeks for a reply. Smartphones mean we don't need to wait for a cab or a table at a restaurant. Movies and TV play immediately. Unfortunately, we are now becoming much worse at waiting for things and social media is in part making this issue worse.

8 Time to stop?

On the one hand, social media makes our world more connected than ever. On the other hand, it also makes many people feel more anxious about their own image, creates false friendship groups, and many people are less patient. People can be so focused on their online lives that they lose time and sleep and ignore the world around them. People who give up social media can feel more connected to their work, their relationships, their family, their friends, and themselves. Perhaps we all need to take a break.

GLOSSARY

popularity contest (n) an attempt to be more popular and liked than other people

C Global reading

1 Read *Social media society* quickly and check your predictions.

> Arguments can be in the same paragraph, or a positive paragraph can be followed by a negative paragraph. You can identify an argument with key words and phrases such as: *some people believe, many people argue, however.*

2 Read the text and highlight the phrases that show that an argument or opinion is being presented.

3 Match each argument with a paragraph in the text.

A Social media is good for younger and older people. ___

B Social media means people spend more time on their own. ___

C Social media lets younger people socialize. ___

D Social media makes people feel bad when they compare themselves to other people. ___

E Social media makes us want everything now. ___

F Social media makes us have false friendships. ___

D Close reading

Read the text again. Do these statements agree or disagree with the opinions in the text or is no information given? Write *Y* (Yes), *N* (No), or *NG* (Not Given).

1 Social media is one of the main changes in modern society. _____

2 Hikikomori is just a Japanese problem. _____

3 Teenagers are not addicted to social media. _____

4 Celebrity profiles show stars' real lives. _____

5 People post photos to get attention. _____

6 Social media does not affect other parts of our life. _____

7 Social media has caused people to lose their jobs. _____

8 Technology has made us less able to wait. _____

E Critical thinking

1 Decide if you agree or disagree with each of these statements.

1 Social media makes people feel anxious and depressed.

2 Social media makes people want everything now.

2 Compare your opinions in groups and give your reasons.

Vocabulary development

Phrases for giving opinions

1 Which words below are used to:

  a mean "I think"

  b emphasize how strongly you believe something

  c show which side of the argument you are on?

> agree with   completely   disagree   I feel   I find
> in my experience   in my opinion   to some extent

2 Choose the best way to complete the sentences.

  1 Sorry, but I **disagree / agree** with you. I think it's rude to arrive late.

  2 I **find / agree with** it strange to eat out so late, but it's normal here.

  3 I **completely / feel** agree with you. It's fine to use your phone on the train.

  4 I think you're right **completely / to some extent**, but perhaps the language has changed.

  5 **In my experience / Completely** older people really aren't any more polite than younger people.

  6 I **to some extent / agree with** you. I think people should always remove their shoes before they go into someone's house.

  7 **Disagree / In my opinion**, polite behavior is always changing and people need to change.

  8 I **feel / agree with** it is fine to e-mail during meetings.

3 Discuss these opinions with a partner. Try to use the phrases and words from Exercise 1.

  1 Polite behavior is the same throughout the world.

  2 You should judge someone who is late for a job interview.

  3 Technology has made people ruder.

Academic words

1 Match the words in bold with the correct definitions.

1 **appropriate** (adj)
2 **attitude** (n)
3 **factor** (n)
4 **ignore** (v)
5 **network** (n)
6 **reaction** (n)
7 **trend** (n)
8 **version** (n)

a one of the things that influence whether an event happens or the way that it happens
b someone's opinions or feelings about something
c a large system with many connected parts
d to not listen to someone or to not give something attention
e a gradual change or development
f suitable or right for the situation or purpose
g the way that you feel or behave as a result of something that happens
h a form of something, such as a computer program, that is different to other ones

2 Complete the paragraph with words from Exercise 1.

When you create an online profile it's important to check that the content is 1_____ for work. This is because there is a growing 2_____ for people outside of your 3_____ to check your profile. One 4_____ employers consider before interviewing someone is their online profile. An employer's 5_____ to your profile can decide whether you get an interview or not. Despite having good qualifications, you might not get an interview if your online profile suggests you don't have a good 6_____ to work. Your social media image cannot just be a 7_____ of yourself for your friends. Other people will check it carefully. If you 8_____ this fact you might not get the job you want.

3 Discuss these questions with a partner.

1 What type of social media do you use?
2 Do you think about how appropriate your social profile is for future employers?
3 Are there any social media trends that you think are not polite?

Writing model

You are going to study discourse markers of contrast and comparison and techniques for writing balanced opinions. You are then going to use these to write a paragraph to answer the question:

"Young people today are not polite. To what extent do you agree or disagree?"

A Analyze

Complete the table with arguments from the model that answers the question: *"Some people think that social media has had a negative effect on young people's behavior. To what extent do you agree?"*

Agree	Disagree

B Model

On the one hand, some people think social media sites have affected children's behavior. They argue that it has affected family relationships and made children less social with adults. Another factor that makes parents feel anxious is that they cannot read their children's posts on social media pages. On the other hand, some people feel it gives children more opportunities to socialize with their friends. Many parents nowadays do not allow children to play outside so much, however, rather than ignore their friends, children now have an online network. I agree with the second opinion because it is important for children to have close friendships and even before social media many children had difficult relationships with their parents.

1 Read the model answer and answer the questions.

   1 What phrases are used to introduce opinions?

   2 Is the agree or disagree side of the argument presented first?

2 Which side does the writer agree with?

3 Discuss these questions with a partner.

   1 Do you agree with the opinions in the paragraph? Why / why not?

   2 What other new things have affected young people in society?

   3 Have these changes made young people more or less polite?

Grammar

Discourse markers of contrast and comparison

Discourse markers of contrast

We use discourse markers of contrast to show differences between two points. *However* and *whereas* go between the points being contrasted. *Although*, *while*, and *though* go before the two points being contrasted. We use *on the one hand* and *on the other hand* together.

*Social media is great for communication. **However,** it does have some negative effects.*

*In the past, we shared photos with a few people **whereas** today we share them with hundreds.*

***Although** social media has some benefits, there are also many negatives.*

***While** we communicate more, we spend less time talking in person.*

***Though** we have many connections, a lot are not really friends.*

***On the one hand,** social media makes us feel connected. **On the other hand,** it also makes us feel judged.*

Discourse markers of comparison

We use discourse markers of comparison to show how two things are similar. *Equally* and *like* usually go between the points being compared. *Both* goes before the points being compared.

*Social media can make people feel positive. **Equally,** it can make them feel stressed.*

*Comments, **like** photos, present an image of ourselves.*

***Both** older and younger people are using social media more often.*

---

1   Read the sentences. Decide if they show *S* (Similarities) or *D* (Differences).

   1   However, in Japan tipping is not expected in any situation and may even create a difficult situation by offending someone. ___

   2   Although most people agree these behaviors are polite, there is a big difference in politeness between the generations. ___

   3   While most children learn to read easily, some need extra help. ___

   4   Many younger people are likely to consider this as acceptable whereas older people are much more likely to find this rude. ___

   5   Equally, social media is now a popularity contest. ___

   6   Though social media helps us to communicate with other people, it can also change how we see ourselves. ___

   7   Both companies and people use social media to create an image. ___

   8   Normal people, like celebrities, often share photos on social media. ___

   9   On the one hand, social media makes our world more connected than ever. On the other hand, it also makes many people feel less sociable. ___

2 Circle the best word to complete each sentence.

1 ___ older and younger generations are affected by social media.

   a Though   b Like   c Both

2 Some people believe younger people are not as polite. ___, it is simply because polite behavior changes over time.

   a Likewise   b However   c Though

3 ___ e-mail is an efficient way to communicate, some companies are using other messaging services.

   a However   b Although   c Both

4 ___ social media sites have some advantages, there are also many negatives.

   a While   b Similarly   c Both

5 ___ giving a business card with two hands is polite in some cultures, this is not the case in all.

   a However   b Like   c Although

6 Social media started only a few years ago. ___, nearly a third of the world uses it today.

   a Equally   b Though   c However

7 In southern Europe, meetings are likely to start with a long conversation not related to work. ___ in Latin America, it is common to speak about your private life first, before discussing business.

   a Both   b Equally   c However

3 Rewrite the sentences using the discourse markers in parentheses.

1 Students find cell phones in the classroom rude. Teachers find cell phones in the classroom rude. (**both**)

_____

2 Talking loudly on the train is rude. It is often necessary. (**however**)

_____

3 People should not worry about "likes" and negative comments on their social media. (**similarly**)

_____

4 People need to stay connected through social media. They should limit their use. (**on the one hand / on the other hand**)

_____

4 Discuss with a partner whether you agree or disagree with the sentences from Exercise 3. Give reasons for your opinions.

Writing skill

A paragraph that gives a balanced opinion is usually structured like this:
- Present one viewpoint (the opposite of the writer's opinion).
- Give supporting reason(s).
- Introduce an alternative viewpoint (matches the writer's opinion).
- Give supporting reason(s).
- Conclude with own viewpoint.

1 Put the phrases for giving opinions into the correct column in the table.

Another argument is   I feel that   In my experience   In my opinion
One argument is   Others feel that   Some people believe

Stating the first viewpoint	Stating an alternative viewpoint	Giving the author's viewpoint

2 Look at the structure in the skills box. Put the sentences in the correct order (1–8).

a They argue that this is because technology has made them unable to interact with others. ___

b However, other people feel that young people are equally polite today. ___

c Some people think that young people are not as polite today as they were in the past. _1_

d Technology changes how we live our lives and as a result it also changes what we think is rude or polite. ___

e In my opinion, while these behaviors might be thought of as rude now, it is likely they will be seen as normal behavior in the future. ___

f Lastly, some people find their behavior rude on public transportation when conversations on cell phones are too loud. ___

g For example, young people behave in an inappropriate way by using technology in situations that are not acceptable such as during a meal or a meeting. ___

h Firstly, this behavior is only considered rude by a few people. ___

3 Label the function of each sentence.

a viewpoint   a reason   personal opinion

4 Which view do you agree with? Why? Discuss with a partner.

Writing task

You are going to study discourse markers of contrast and comparison and techniques for writing balanced opinions. You are then going to write a paragraph to answer the question:

"Young people today are not polite. To what extent do you agree or disagree?"

Brainstorm

Complete the brainstorm below with your ideas.

Agree	Disagree

Plan

1 Choose two arguments to agree and think of an example for each.

2 Choose two arguments to disagree and think of an example for each.

3 Which arguments do you agree with the most?

Write

Using your answers to the questions above, write a paragraph answering the essay question. Use some comparison and contrast phrases to connect your ideas. Pay attention to the organization of your arguments. Your text should be about 100 words long.

Share

Exchange paragraphs with a partner. Look at the checklist on page 189 and provide feedback to your partner.

Rewrite and edit

Read your partner's comments. What could you change to make your writing better? Revise your text, then check it for errors. Think about:

- discourse markers of contrast and comparison
- giving a balanced opinion.

Write the final draft.

Review

Wordlist

MACMILLAN DICTIONARY

Vocabulary preview			
anxious (adj) **	get attention (phrase) ***	opinion (n) ***	site (n) **
behavior (n) ***	hurt (v) ***	page (n) ***	smile (v) ***
consider (v) ***	judge (v) ***	post (v) **	social media (n) *
cruel (adj) **	manners (n) ***	rude (adj) **	tip (v) **
Vocabulary development			
agree with (phr v)	disagree (v) **	find (v) ***	in my opinion (phrase)
completely (adv) ***	feel (v) ***	in my experience (phrase)	to some extent (phrase)
Academic words			
appropriate (adj) **	factor (n) ***	network (n) ***	trend (n) ***
attitude (n) ***	ignore (v) **	reaction (n) ***	version (n) ***

Academic words review

Complete the sentences with the words in the box.

appropriate	ignore	network	trends	version

1   The police interviewed both suspects. One suspect told one story, and the other told a completely different _____ of events.
2   It is important to have a _____ of colleagues to share information and experiences with.
3   Don't _____ the advice of older people. They have a lot of experience to offer young people.
4   I like looking at fashion magazines to see the latest _____.
5   When applying for a job, it is important to use _____ language and not be too informal.

Unit review

Reading 1   ☐   I can use topic sentences to understand the main ideas.

Reading 2   ☐   I can identify arguments and opinions in a text.

Study skill   ☐   I can use reflective learning journals to support my studying.

Vocabulary   ☐   I can use words and phrases for giving my opinion.

Grammar   ☐   I can use discourse markers of contrast and comparison.

Writing   ☐   I can write a balanced opinion paragraph.

Discussion point

Discuss with a partner.

1 Look at the infographic about seasons for growing fruit and vegetables in parts of America. Do you grow these foods in your country?

2 What foods grow in your country during different times of year?

3 Do you think it is important to eat foods that are in season? Why?

FOOD SEASONS

SPRING

SUMMER

WINTER

FALL

VIDEO

ARABIC SUSHI

Before you watch

Work with a partner. Which of the following opinions matches yours the best? Why?

1 I prefer to eat food from my own culture.

2 I prefer to eat food from other cultures.

3 I like to eat food that is a mix of different cultures.

UNIT AIMS

READING 1 Completing a summary of main ideas
READING 2 Understanding synonyms
STUDY SKILL Tricks for getting started

VOCABULARY Adjectives for describing food
GRAMMAR Relative clauses
WRITING Using compound sentences

Fruit and vegetable market in Turkey.

While you watch

Read the questions and then watch the video. Check (✓) the correct answers.

1 What flavor does the food have?

☐ Chinese   ☐ Japanese

☐ Middle Eastern ☐ Italian

2 What happens when Western people try the food?

☐ They try more   ☐ They try more
   Arabic food.   Japanese food.

3 What do the customers think?

☐ They like it.   ☐ They are confused by it.

After you watch

Answer the questions with a partner.

1 Do you think this restaurant idea would be popular in your country?

Yes, because ...   *No, because ...*

2 Is the food from your country popular around the world?

Yes, my country's food ...

No, my country's food ...

3 What international food do you think would mix well with your culture's food?

I think it would mix well with ... because ...

The food of Indonesia

A Vocabulary preview

Find the words in the text and match them with the definitions.

1 **farming** (n)
2 **food stall** (n)
3 **groceries** (n)
4 **herbs and spices** (n)
5 **industry** (n)
6 **plant** (v)
7 **processed food** (n)
8 **soil** (n)

a the substance on the surface of the Earth in which plants grow
b food changed from its natural state
c growing crops or producing animal products
d things used to add flavor to food
e to put trees, seeds, etc. in the ground to grow
f the food you regularly buy in a store
g a large table or a small building that is open at the front, used for selling food
h the people and organizations involved in producing goods

B Before you read

Previewing a text

Look at the picture and heading. What is the text's purpose?

a To give an overview of the Indonesian food industry
b To compare the Indonesian food industry with food in the rest of the world

C Global reading

Completing a summary of main ideas

> Summaries give an overview of the main ideas in a text. Read the topic sentences and identify the supporting information and important words to help you summarize the main ideas.

1 Skim *The food of Indonesia* and check (✓) the things that are mentioned in the text.

challenges in the past   challenges today   changes to diet and shopping
changes to jobs   local dishes   money for farmers   plants and crops

2 Use your answers from Exercise 1 to complete a summary of the text.

Indonesia has a lot of rain and sunshine and produces different [1]_____.
These traditionally influence the food and a lot of herbs and spices are used in
[2]_____. However, [3]_____ and [4]_____ habits are
changing. Today people eat more processed foods. People often buy groceries in
local stores, but they also use supermarkets. One of the main [5]_____
for the food industry [6]_____ is the increasing population. It means
more foods have to be imported.

The food of Indonesia

1 Situated in a warm, tropical region, Indonesia has a lot of rain and sunshine and therefore has the perfect climate for a long growing season. The country also has large areas of good-quality soil. Both factors make Indonesia an excellent region for a successful farming economy. A large percentage of the population works in the farming industry and the country gets a lot of income from this. There is a large range of farms, but most belong to three types: small farms growing rice for domestic use, small farms growing crops for export, and large, foreign-owned or privately-owned farms that also mostly export food.

2 Indonesia's climate makes it ideal for planting and growing most popular crops. Indonesia is one of the world's largest producers of many different kinds of food. It is a known producer of palm oil and spices like cloves and cinnamon. It is also one of the biggest producers of other key foods consumers frequently buy such as cocoa, coffee, and tea. Growing plants to eat is obviously important, yet many farmers also plant other crops of high value such as natural rubber.

3 The farming industry is clearly important for the country's economy, however, it has also influenced the local food culture and customs. Indonesia has a long history of cooking with herbs and spices. The Betawi, who are a local group in the region of Jakarta, are responsible for many of the street foods. Kerak Telor, which is possibly their most famous dish, is made of rice, coconut, onions, shrimp, and egg and fried into a cake. With thousands of street food stalls selling dishes for under one U.S. dollar they form an important part of the economy.

4 As Indonesia has become richer and more urban the local diets have gradually changed. In particular, the amount of dairy, meat, and sugar people eat has grown. Many of these products and other processed foods and drink are often imported. A lot of people still prefer to shop in traditional local stores for their groceries, but supermarkets are selling an increasing amount of food to urban people. These stores mostly sell processed foods and often have better refrigerators to keep the dairy and meat products people demand.

5 As lifestyles and diets change there are many challenges facing the Indonesian food industry. In the past, the country produced enough rice and sugar for everyone, but now it needs to import these foods. An increasing population, more land being used for crops people do not eat, and growing industries are all placing pressure on the future of food in Indonesia.

GLOSSARY

imported (adj) brought into your country from another country

rubber (n) a strong material made from a tree and that bends easily

Man frying Kerak Telor.

Scanning

D Close reading

Read the text again. Write *T* (True), *F* (False), or *NG* (Not Given) for each sentence.

1   Very few people now work in farming in Indonesia. ___
2   Indonesia does not produce any meat products. ___
3   Herbs and spices are quite new in Indonesian cooking. ___
4   People now eat more processed foods. ___
5   Indonesia can produce all of the rice and sugar it needs today. ___

E Critical thinking

Discuss these questions in a group.

1   What changes in diet have there been in Indonesia? Have you had similar changes in diet in your country?

   The diet in Indonesia has changed to …
   The diet in my country …

2   Why do you think people eat more processed foods today? What health problems might it cause?

   People's diets have changed because …
   Eating more processed foods can cause …

Study skills Tricks for getting started

Write down everything you know and think about the topic.

Free writing

- Give yourself three minutes
- Write as fast as you can – all your ideas – as they arrive
- Don't bother about sentences or punctuation – it's only a draft to get going

Free association

© Stella Cottrell (2013)

1 Read *Tricks for getting started*. Choose one of the ideas below and complete a free writing task on the topic you chose.

> food production   healthy eating and diets   junk food   popular snacks

2 Find another student who chose the same topic as you. Compare your notes. Add any ideas you like from your partner's list to your list.

3 Choose one of the other topics from Exercise 1. This time complete the free association task from the box.

4 Find another student who chose the same topic as you. Compare your notes. Add any ideas you like from your partner's list to your notes.

Farming in extremes

A Vocabulary preview

1 Complete the questions with the words in the box.

> artificial   claim   cost   crops   environmental   human   locally   pollute

1 What foods are grown _____ in your region?
2 Do you believe it when people _____ that climate change is not happening?
3 Do you think _____ behavior needs to change to protect the environment?
4 Would you eat different _____ to protect the environment?
5 What _____ damage is caused when food is imported?
6 What foods are grown using _____ light or heat in your country?
7 Does local food or imported food _____ more in your country?
8 What things about your diet _____ the environment the most?

2 Discuss the questions from Exercise 1 with a partner.

Preparing to read

B Before you read

Discuss these questions with a partner.

1 What foods do you eat regularly?

   I often have …   I eat … regularly …

2 How much of your food is grown locally?

   A lot of my food is grown locally because …

   Not much of it is grown locally because …

3 What makes it difficult to grow some foods in your country?

   It is difficult to grow … because …

C Global reading

Skimming

Read the text quickly and choose the best alternative title.

1 The food we eat
2 Farming today
3 Farming solutions

FARMING IN *extremes*

1 Harder times

It is thought that the world's population will reach about nine billion in 2050. That's around two billion more than now. When you consider that there are around one billion people in the world already living in difficult times due to a lack of food, then the future is worrying. Also, with the increasing difficulty facing the world due to human numbers and climate change, many wonder how we will feed this larger population without destroying the planet.

2 The damage farming does

Surprisingly, agriculture is one of the biggest causes of global warming. This comes from some of the crops and animals we farm, such as cows and rice farms. It also comes from the chemicals we use to fight diseases and to encourage plants to grow more quickly. Farming also uses a lot of water. This water and the chemicals we use to grow our crops means farming causes a lot of pollution to lakes, rivers, and seas. As our population grows we also cut down more trees. Clearly, how we farm and use the food we produce cannot continue in this way, but what can be done to make farming better and more environmentally friendly?

3 Grow and use food with less waste

Many farms around the world do not produce the volume of crops that they could. Of course, they should not be farmed too much so that the soil is damaged, but they can be grown in a better way. For example, traditional farming often plants different crops next to each other. The amount grown of each is then reduced. Many traditional farms also waste water. Finally, local farmers do not always have access to the best seeds. The best seeds are not affected by diseases and produce higher amounts of crops. Also, much of the food farmed now is wasted rather than used. The United Nations claims that about one third of the food produced for people to eat is not eaten. The cost of this is about one trillion dollars of food wasted each year. People in rich countries waste nearly the same amount of food as the whole of sub-Saharan Africa produces.

GLOSSARY

seed (n) the part of a plant that is used to grow more of the same plant

4 Change diets

One way to reduce environmental effects of the food we produce is to change our diets and what we grow. Changing the food we eat to more fruit and vegetables and less meat could be one way to make certain that we can produce enough food to feed the planet. Much of the food we grow is fed to animals, used as fuel, or used in other products. Farming animals also uses much more water. By changing our eating habits through eating less meat we could actually make better use of the land available to us for farming.

5 Unusual solutions—seawater and sun

Since many people do not want to change their diet, or have not considered changing it, farmers are looking for unusual solutions to produce the food we need. This is especially true in places where they already have problems with a lack of water or poor soil quality. Artificial conditions are created to grow the food. For example, at one farm in Australia, they are producing tomatoes by using solar power to remove salt from the seawater. The tomatoes then grow in greenhouses kept cool by seawater in the summer and made hotter by solar power in the winter.

6 Farming the desert

Many countries are facing the challenges of high birth rates increasing the population and land being covered in desert. This means much of the food is bought abroad and transporting it adds to the problem of global warming. Countries have tried different solutions to this problem. In Egypt, people have tried to develop the desert into farmland. This involves using underground water or taking water from the river Nile. In Qatar, they hope to grow a large amount of their own fruit and vegetables within the next few years. Computer technology means temperatures, water levels, and light can all now be changed to create a range of perfect growing conditions. While an expensive solution, it is one that reduces the damage to the environment and produces more local food.

7 Can we meet the challenges?

Each country faces different challenges to produce food. Some need to think about developing the technology to grow crops in difficult conditions. Others, perhaps, need to look at trying to change people's diets to reduce the amount of meat eaten. The whole world also needs to grow crops in a way that reduces the damage to the environment. Otherwise we may have even less good-quality soil and a warmer climate in which to try to feed everyone.

GLOSSARY

solar power (n) electricity created using energy from the sun

D Close reading

> We use synonyms to avoid repeating a noun to make our language more varied and interesting. It is important to understand what these synonyms refer to in order to fully understand a text. Looking for synonyms can help you identify repeated ideas and the main topic of a section.

1 Read *Farming in extremes*. Find the synonyms or phrases with a similar meaning to these words.

Paragraph 1 – population   ___*people*___   ___*human numbers*___

Paragraph 2 – agriculture   _____   _____

Paragraph 3 – produced   _____   _____

Paragraph 4 – diets   _____   _____

2 Replace the words in bold using synonyms from paragraphs 5–7.

1 In hot areas farmers now **take away** the salt from seawater.

2 A lot of the food comes from **foreign countries**.

3 Some people think it is a good idea **to lower** the amount of meat we eat.

3 Read *Farming in extremes* again. Match each sentence (1–5) with a group (A–C) below. You can use any letter more than once.

1 They traditionally waste space and water. ___

2 They say that one third of the food we grow is wasted. ___

3 There will be much more of them by 2050. ___

4 They are now thinking of using computers to help them work in Qatar. ___

5 They will need to change what they eat in the future. ___

A Farmers

B Scientists and official groups

C The general population

E Critical thinking

Think about the ideas from *The food of Indonesia* and *Farming in extremes* and discuss these questions in a group.

1 What traditional foods eaten in your country are imported from other countries?

Nowadays we usually import most of our … from …

2 Do you think you could reduce the amount of processed foods you eat? Why / why not?

I could stop eating a lot of processed foods like …

Vocabulary development

Adjectives for describing food

1 Match the words in bold with the correct definitions.

1	**bitter** (adj)	a	tasting strong and sharp, not sweet
2	**creamy** (adj)	b	containing salt or tasting like salt
3	**frozen** (adj)	c	with a strong hot flavor
4	**juicy** (adj)	d	with a flavor you enjoy
5	**salty** (adj)	e	thick, soft, often containing a dairy product
6	**smelly** (adj)	f	unpleasant when you breathe in through your nose
7	**spicy** (adj)	g	extremely cold and stored at a very low temperature
8	**tasty** (adj)	h	containing a lot of liquid

2 Complete the sentences with words from Exercise 1.

1 _____ yoghurt is a popular alternative to ice cream.

2 A: What do these chilies on the menu mean?

B: They show you how _____ a dish is. Three is the strongest.

3 This apple is really sweet and _____.

4 _____ food can be bad for people trying to lose weight because of the amount of fat.

5 I always try the food first. Sometimes it's really _____ so you do not need to add any more seasoning.

6 I really like this cheese, but it's so _____, the room stinks!

7 This food isn't very _____. You need to add something to give it some flavor.

8 I always add sugar and milk to my coffee otherwise it's too _____.

3 Discuss these questions with a partner.

1 Do you prefer sweet or salty snacks?

2 Which adjectives best describe your favorite food?

Academic words

1 Match the words in bold with the correct definitions.

1	**approach** (n)	a	relating to the country being talked about and not another country
2	**chemical** (n)		
3	**consumer** (n)	b	a way or method of doing something
4	**contribution** (n)	c	to sell something to another country
5	**domestic** (adj)	d	money that someone gets from work or investments
6	**export** (v)	e	a person who buys something
7	**global** (adj)	f	including or affecting the whole world
8	**income** (n)	g	something used in chemistry or produced by a process involving chemistry
		h	something you do or share that helps change things

2 Complete the sentences with words from Exercise 1 in the correct form.

1 We _____ a lot of food around the world, especially bananas, tea, and coffee.

2 _____ are shopping online, rather than in stores.

3 Many farmers use a _____ such as a fertilizer to help plants grow.

4 Diet and lifestyle choices have made a significant _____ to many modern health problems.

5 One _____ to solving the problem of not enough food is to change people's diets.

6 _____ warming is a problem facing the whole world.

7 The _____ economy is mostly farming and tourism.

8 Our country's _____ comes mainly from exporting oil.

3 Discuss these questions with a partner.

1 Do you think consumers worry about where their food comes from?
I think consumers worry because …
I don't think consumers worry because …

2 What does your country mainly export?
My country mainly exports …

3 What does your country produce mainly for the domestic market?
For the domestic market, my country mainly produces …

Writing model

You are going to learn about using relative clauses and writing compound sentences. You are then going to use these to write a paragraph describing food production in your country.

A Analyze

Use the bold words in the brainstorm in the correct form to complete the model answer.

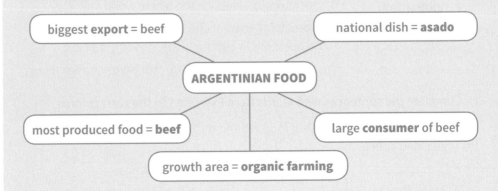

biggest **export** = beef

national dish = **asado**

ARGENTINIAN FOOD

most produced food = **beef**

large **consumer** of beef

growth area = **organic farming**

B Model

Nearly half of the land in Argentina is used to produce meat. [1]_____ is by far the most important of these products and is one of Argentina's most important [2]_____. The country is also one of the largest [3]_____ per person of beef in the world. An [4]_____, which is the local name for a barbecue, is one of the most popular ways to eat meat. It is the national dish and it is often served with a spicy chimichurri sauce. Currently, [5]_____, which is farming without the use of chemicals, is a small but growing area. Argentina is one of the biggest organic farming countries in the world and companies export nearly all of these foods.

1 Match the sentences from the text with the topics.

   1 Sentences 1–3 ___   a A national dish

   2 Sentences 4–5 ___   b A new area in farming

   3 Sentences 6–7 ___   c The most important food in farming

2 Discuss these questions with a partner.

   1 Are different regions of your country known for different foods?

   2 What national dishes are these used in?

   3 What changes have there been in the food produced in your country? Is this because of local changes in diet or for export?

Grammar

Relative clauses

We use relative clauses to describe or give extra information about an object, person, or place.

We use **who** to describe people.	People **who live in urban areas** now have different diets.
We use **that** and **which** for things.	The farms **that** we visited use new approaches to farming. Crops **which need a tropical climate** grow well in Indonesia.
We use **where** to describe locations and places.	More land **where farming takes place** is now being used for industry.

Some relative clauses give information to explain the specific place, object, or person the writer is talking about. These are **defining relative clauses**.

*Products **which are environmentally friendly** try to limit the damage they do to the environment.*

Another type of relative clause is a **non-defining relative clause**. This type of clause does not tell you which one. It tells you more information about the thing already named or defined. Non-defining clauses use commas (, ,) at the start and end of the clause.

*The Betawi, **who are a local group in the region of Jakarta**, are responsible for many of the street foods.*

1 Underline the relative clause. Decide if the clause is defining or non-defining.

1 Common foods which are grown in this country include wheat, fruit, and vegetables. _____

2 Farmers who sell in the local market always sell seasonal crops. _____

3 Crumble, which is an English dessert, is made from fruit, flour, sugar, and butter. _____

4 The area on the coast, where many farmers are based, is good for growing crops. _____

5 The food stall owners, who work in this area, must have a license. _____

6 The town where I lived as a teenager is famous for its hot and spicy food. _____

Pomegranate farming in Turkey.

2 Complete the sentences with *who*, *which / that*, or *where*.

1 People _____ lived in the countryside were given a small piece of land to farm.

2 In the past, people lived _____ it was easy to grow their own food.

3 The new kinds of food _____ are popular nowadays are usually processed and unhealthy.

4 The food _____ we eat in my country is usually imported.

5 In hot and dry places, _____ there is little rain, it is often hard to grow food.

6 She thinks people living in the city, _____ are usually richer, do not eat as much fresh fruit and vegetables.

3 Join the sentences using a defining or non-defining relative clause after the subject of each sentence.

1 The East of China has the best farmland. Most people live there.
   The East of China, where most people live, has the best farmland.

2 The people mostly eat fish. They live on small islands.
   _____

3 Bottled water is more expensive than gas. It comes from other countries.
   _____

4 The dish comes from the north of the country. It is made from rice, fish, herbs, and spices.
   _____

5 The places are in the center of the country. They eat more meat.
   _____

Writing skill

A sentence with two or more independent clauses (clauses with a subject and a verb) is a compound sentence. Compound sentences are made by joining the two clauses with a conjunction. For example:

*Japanese food is commonly exported around the world **and** its most famous type of food is sushi.*

*We have a lot of farmland, **but** the country still buys a lot of its food from other countries.*

*The country has a high population and not much land **so** it has to import most of its food.*

While is also used to join independent clauses. As a conjunction, **while** has a similar function to **but**.

***While** fast food is very popular, it is not eaten by everyone.*

Since is also used to join independent clauses and has a similar meaning to **because**.

*Our country does not produce much food **since** it is too hot here for most things to grow.*

1 Choose the correct conjunction to complete these compound sentences.

   1 **Since / While** it is more environmentally friendly to eat locally grown food, many countries spend millions of dollars buying foods from thousands of miles away.

   2 Farming underground would have some advantages, **but / and** one difficulty is that it would need to use artificial light.

   3 These stores mostly sell processed foods **and / so** have better refrigerators to store the milk and meat products people demand.

   4 The world's population is growing, **yet / so** we need more space to produce food.

2 Rewrite the sentences as compound sentences.

   1 Many people's lives have become better. Their diets have become worse.

   2 We need more food to feed everyone. The population is growing.

   3 Previously, people lived on small farms. They ate the food they grew.

   4 It rains a lot. The country grows most of its own food.

   5 We are eating more food. We are growing less food ourselves.

3 Use the conjunctions in the skills box to write four compound sentences about your favorite foods in your country.

Writing task

Use relative clauses and compound sentences to write a paragraph describing food production in your country.

Brainstorm

Complete the brainstorm below.

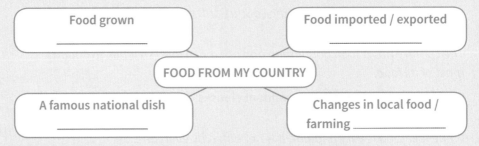

Food grown
_____

Food imported / exported
_____

FOOD FROM MY COUNTRY

A famous national dish
_____

Changes in local food / farming _____

Plan

Answer the following questions as you plan your description.

1   What are the main foods produced in your country?
2   What local dish are these foods used in?
3   What foods does your country import and export?
4   What do you think will happen to food production in the future in your country?
5   What other information can you think of about food in your country?

Write

Using your answers to the questions above, write a paragraph about food production in your country. Use some compound sentences with *but, and, so, while,* or *since.* Pay attention to your relative clauses. Your text should be around 100 words long.

Share

Exchange paragraphs with a partner. Look at the checklist on page 189 and provide feedback to your partner.

Rewrite and edit

Read your partner's comments. What could you change to make your writing better? Revise your text, then check it for errors. Think about:

*   the structure of your compound sentences
*   your use of relative clauses.

Write the final draft.

Review

Wordlist

MACMILLAN
DICTIONARY

Vocabulary preview

artificial (adj) **	food stall (n)	plant (v) **
claim (v) ***	groceries (n)	pollute (v) *
cost (n) ***	herbs and spices (n)	processed food (n)
crops (n) **	human (adj) ***	soil (n) ***
environmental (adj) ***	industry (n) ***	
farming (n) *	locally (adv) **	

Vocabulary development

bitter (adj) **	frozen (adj) *	salty (adj)	spicy (adj)
creamy (adj)	juicy (adj)	smelly (adj)	tasty (adj) *

Academic words

approach (n) ***	contribution (n) ***	global (adj) ***
chemical (n) ***	domestic (adj) ***	income (n) ***
consumer (n) ***	export (v) **	

Academic words review

Complete the sentences with the words in the box.

attitude	exports	factor	global	income

1 Success in life depends as much on your _____ as on your qualifications.
2 India _____ gem stones, refined mineral fuels, vehicles, machinery, medicines and chemicals to many countries.
3 The amount you earn each year is your annual _____.
4 Rising unemployment was a major _____ in the country's economic problems.
5 The importance of recycling plastic is a _____ concern.

Unit review

Reading 1	☐	I can complete a summary of the main ideas in a text.
Reading 2	☐	I can recognize and understand synonyms in a text.
Study skill	☐	I can use tricks for getting started to help me brainstorm ideas.
Vocabulary	☐	I can use adjectives for describing food.
Grammar	☐	I can use relative clauses with *who*, *that / which,* and *where.*
Writing	☐	I use compound sentences to make my writing more interesting.

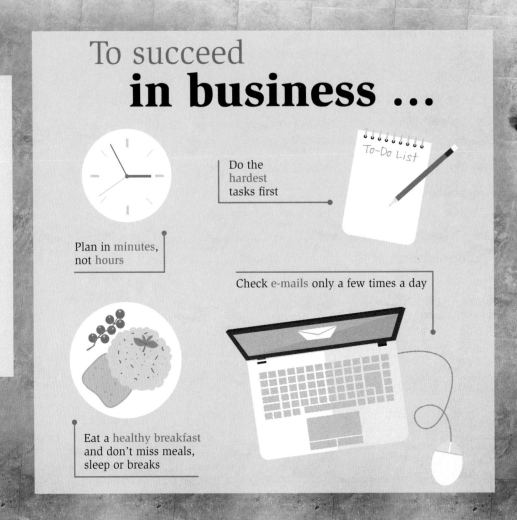

To succeed
in business ...

Plan in minutes, not hours

Do the hardest tasks first

To-Do List

Check e-mails only a few times a day

Eat a healthy breakfast and don't miss meals, sleep or breaks

Discussion point

Discuss with a partner.

1 Which points in the infographic do you think are most useful for people in business?

2 What other things do you think help people become successful in business?

3 How could these tips help people in other areas of their life? For example, studying.

VIDEO

CREATIVE

YOUNG
ENTREPRENEURS

Before you watch

Work with a partner. What do most people want to do after they finish college?

1 Start their own company

2 Work for a large company

3 Work for a small private company

UNIT AIMS

READING 1 Identifying supporting details
READING 2 Signposting
STUDY SKILL What are recruiters looking for?

VOCABULARY Business verbs
GRAMMAR Modals of obligation and necessity
WRITING Writing an introduction

Modern business meeting.

While you watch

Read the statements and then watch the video. Choose the correct option to complete the sentences.

1 A lot of China's young people want **an office job / to be entrepreneurs**.

2 Song left his job because he **was bored / wanted more money**.

3 Cui Ernan thinks starting a business and making money **is / isn't** something everyone can do.

4 Jack Ma and Ma Huateng were very **lucky / experienced**.

After you watch

Answer the questions with a partner.

1 Do lots of students you know in your country try to start their own companies?

No, in my country …

Yes, they do. Many people …

2 Is it difficult to find a job after college?

Yes, it is, because …

No, it isn't, because …

3 What type of businesses do people try to start?

Lots of people want to open …

How much is it worth?

A Vocabulary preview

1 Complete the sentences with the words in the box.

> brand   customer service   excellence   logo   quality   trust   value

1 Do you _____ sales staff or do you think they are just trying to make money?

2 How important is good _____ to you? Would you use a company if staff were rude to you?

3 What _____ of clothing is the most popular in your country?

4 _____ in customer service and perfect support is the most important thing for a business. To what extent do you agree with this?

5 What do you think adds _____ to businesses? What makes a company successful?

6 A company _____ is something people should remember. Which symbols do you know the best?

7 What is more important for you, good- _____ products or cheap products?

2 Discuss the questions in Exercise 1 with a partner.

B Before you read

Preparing to read

Think about your favorite clothing brands and technology products. Tell your partner about them and why you like them.

C Global reading

Identifying main ideas

1 Match these questions with paragraphs 2–4.

1 What do brands say about people?

2 How important is customer service?

3 How important are quality products?

2 Using the questions from Exercise 1, which paragraph would you expect to see these words in?

> apologize   image   quality   reputation   rude   standard

3 Scan the text and check your predictions.

How much is it worth?

1 When people think of a valuable company they tend to think of how much the company is worth in terms of money. Every year, companies report how much money they have made and directors' salaries and bonuses also depend on the money brought in. While this may be what the company owners value, to build a successful business, you need to think about the things customers value. Customer service, well-known brands, and quality products are all ways in which we can judge the value of a company.

2 Successful businesses know that they must provide good customer service as they will be judged by it. For instance, rude customer service, unlike a faulty product, cannot be returned. Of course, you can apologize, but the damage has already been done and sales could decline as a result. Excellence in customer service is very important because the cost of attracting a new customer is much higher than the cost of keeping an existing one. Which means increasing the number of customers you keep can make your company more profitable. If a company has a unique product, this is perhaps less of an issue, but when two or more companies are selling basically the same product, the success of the company depends on how well its customers are treated. This means that companies need to communicate clearly, fix problems quickly, personalize the sales experience, and employ the right people.

3 One way to make a company successful is to build a strong brand. This is because people associate a certain standard and quality with brands and this builds trust. It seems people are willing to spend a lot of money on good-quality products even when they do not need them. Your laptop shows the time. Your cell phone displays the time. So does your car's dashboard, the screen in the subway, and millions of other items. A watch is no longer essential, so why are these expensive items still popular? Watches have been rebranded so that they are no longer simply tools for telling the time. They show what kind of a person the wearer is, represent tradition,

and use technology. Much like cars, they are used by people to show their status.

4 Brands are also important because they say something about who we are. When people think of a brand, the values associated with it come to people's minds. Whether a brand is seen as family-friendly, popular, or user-friendly is important because we like to buy brands that represent how we like to present ourselves to others. If people see themselves as creative then they are more likely to buy creative products that match their self-image. One way companies build these values and their reputation is through their logo and by linking it to particular celebrities. If a famous person is known for being a good family person, then a company may use them to help link this characteristic to their products.

5 Companies, when well-managed, can create value by focusing on quality products and building their brand. With clever marketing and by maintaining good customer service a company can push up its value a long way beyond what it would be otherwise.

D Close reading

> Supporting details are used to give the reader a clearer understanding of the topic. You can identify these using a number of key phrases.
>
> **Examples:**
>
> *such as, for instance, one example is*
>
> **Reasons:**
>
> *because, due to, in order to*
>
> **Explanations:**
>
> *in other words, which means*

1 Scan the text to complete the supporting details.

   1 You can return a broken product, but you cannot return _____.

   2 It is more expensive to attract _____ than to keep old ones.

   3 A lot of companies sell the same _____.

   4 People are willing to spend a lot of money on _____ products.

   5 People do not need _____, but they are still popular.

   6 People like to buy brands that represent _____.

2 Look at the main ideas (1–3) below. Match the details 1–6 in Exercise 1 with the main ideas they support.

   1 People link logos and brands to their identities. ___

   2 Good customer service is very important. ___ ___ ___

   3 People value high-quality products. ___ ___

E Critical thinking

1 Which of the ideas in the text do you think adds most value to a company? Customer service, a well-known brand, or quality products? Why do you think this?

   I think … adds most value because …

2 What other things not mentioned in the text do you think add value to a company? Discuss your ideas with a partner. Think about:

   company hours

   happy and reliable employees

   quick service

   other …

Study skills | What are recruiters looking for?

Although employers still value academic and specialist skills, they also look for a wider range of experience and generic skills, especially 'soft skills'. Employers value soft skills in the following areas:

1 Managing people: people skills

Teamworking; communication skills; customer focus; leadership and ability to support and motivate others; cultural awareness; languages.

2 Managing projects: task management skills

Ability to get on with tasks without close supervision; attention to detail; being logical; applying technology; problem-solving; flexibility; willingness to take risks; solution-focused; work ethic.

© Stella Cottrell (2013)

1 Read *What are recruiters looking for?* Match these skills with the two categories.

| being careful | finishing work on time | leading a team | supporting others |
| working hard | working on your own | working with others | |

Managing people	Managing projects

2 Compare your answers with a partner.

3 Read this student profile. Discuss with a partner how his experience shows examples of soft skills.

Juan is from Spain and he is studying Business at a college in the U.S. He has taken modules in Accounting, Digital Marketing, and English. His assessments have included designing a website, writing a group report, and leading a group presentation. When he graduates he wants to work in online marketing.

4 Think about your own experiences of studying and other areas of your life. What soft skill have you developed that you could tell an employer about? Share your ideas with a partner.

Starting on the path to success?

A Vocabulary preview

Match the words in bold with the correct definitions.

1	**access** (n)	a	to change your ideas or behavior so that you can deal with a new situation
2	**adapt** (v)		
3	**business model** (n)	b	someone who uses money to start businesses.
4	**entrepreneur** (n)	c	a small new company
5	**existing** (adj)	d	already present
6	**make decisions** (phrase)	e	to choose options after thinking carefully
7	**start-up** (n)	f	the way a company is structured to operate
		g	the way people reach or buy a product

B Before you read

Preparing to read

Discuss these questions with a partner.

1 Would you like to be an entrepreneur with your own start-up company?

2 Why do you think so many people decide to start their own companies?

C Global reading

Signposting

> In the introduction, the main idea of a text will be signposted by a sentence that states the main opinion or topic.
>
> To make a transition in the text, writers often signpost new ideas using words such as *firstly*, *secondly*, and *finally*. Paying attention to these can help you understand how a text is organized.

1 Read the introduction to *Starting on the path to success?* only.
   Which sentence tells you the main focus of the text?

2 From the introduction, check (✓) the things you expect the text to cover.

☐ Successful start-ups

☐ The failure of start-ups

☐ The history of traditional businesses

☐ Examples of how businesses can be successful

☐ The most successful entrepreneurs today

3 Read the text and find the following:

1 Two ways in which start-ups can create products (paragraph 2)

2 Three reasons why companies might give people free products (paragraph 3)

3 Three reasons for start-ups failing (paragraph 4)

4 Two additional reasons for start-ups failing (paragraph 5)

STARTING ON
THE PATH TO SUCCESS?

1 It once took a company a long time to be worth a billion dollars. Today dozens of tech start-ups are achieving this level of economic success within their first five years. While successful tech start-ups have the ability to change traditional industries, many are still not successful. Companies should focus on easy access, the use of free content, creating a product people need, and the time it takes to be successful.

2 So what is needed to be a successful start-up? Firstly, you do not have to create a completely new product to sell. One approach many entrepreneurs take is just to improve access to products that already exist. This can be via an online shop, like Amazon, selling and delivering a huge range of products around the world. Another approach is by changing how we use a product. For instance, the industry of streaming movies and TV shows has seen big increases in the last decade. Many previously successful companies have now closed because of their decision to continue to sell the old physical products that people were demanding much less. Knowing when and how to adapt to the changing world is vital—when was the last time you rented a DVD through the mail?

3 Another recent change is the increased demand for free products. Why has this proven to be such a successful concept? Firstly, there is the obvious point that most people like receiving something for free. However, giving everything away for free is clearly not a good business model. The second main reason is that companies can give people a small part of a product for free and then charge for more features. This is called a freemium model. One issue start-ups find difficult is that very few people will have heard of their product or service. By giving a certain amount away for free, you can get people interested and willing to pay for more or further access. Lastly, companies don't need to spend as much on advertising because people are likely to tell their friends and family about free products. If you give people free products or free access for sharing posts on their social media, then you can reach a lot more people both quickly and cheaply.

4 Despite there being some examples of extremely successful start-ups in recent years, the number of start-ups that fail remains high. So why do so many new businesses fail? One reason might be that there isn't a need for the company's product. One priority any new company should have is to solve a problem that exists. For example, online shopping solved the problem that many people just do not have time to shop in stores. Secondly, companies or products fail because it is the wrong product for the time. Minidiscs, which were smaller versions of CDs, did not do well at first because of their cost. Just as the cost became lower, MP3s became popular and people bought them instead. Thirdly, there isn't always space for the product in a crowded industry. When a market is already nearly full it can be very difficult to get customers to notice you. People already have loyalty to a brand and unless you are very different or unique then a business will find it difficult to be a success.

5 There are a number of other key reasons why a start-up business fails. Firstly, many new businesses simply fail because they do not have enough money available. It can be expensive to run a business, especially at first when you have to spend money on fees to advertise your brand. Many small businesses simply run out of money before they become successful. Secondly, and connected to this, building a good brand can take a long time. It can also take a lot of money to build a reputation before a business becomes successful. Airbnb, which found it difficult at first, managed to improve their brand and reputation by using professional photography. Without the time or money to spend in this way, the company might not be successful today. Companies that can survive more than five years have a much higher chance of going on to become successful and profitable businesses.

6 So what makes some start-ups so successful? Understanding what customers want, timing your product correctly, promoting your company cheaply but well, and having enough money to survive the first five years are important for a start-up to be successful. A fantastic idea five years too early will probably fail. A company with a fantastic product but a lack of money will probably fail. Many things need to fall into place at the right time to put you on the path to success.

GLOSSARY

market (n) a particular group of people that a product is sold to

D Close reading

Read *Starting on the path to success?* again. Choose the correct ending for each sentence.

1 Companies often need to
   a grow to be successful.
   b know when to adapt.
   c operate online to be successful.

2 Giving a product away for free may
   a cost a lot of money.
   b save money on advertising.
   c not be possible for start-ups.

3 Minidiscs did not do well because
   a the technology was not very good.
   b it was cheap and had a bad reputation.
   c another product became available.

4 New companies often need
   a support from celebrities to be successful.
   b exciting new products to be successful.
   c time and money to be successful.

E Critical thinking

1 Do you think *Starting on the path to success?* has good advice for entrepreneurs? Why / why not?

2 Why do we see so many new start-ups despite the high chance of failure?

   We see lots of new start-ups because …

3 Would you rather work for a small start-up or a big business? Why?

   I'd rather work for … because …

Vocabulary development

Business verbs

1 Match the words in bold with the correct definitions.

1 **advertise** (v)
2 **communicate** (v)
3 **employ** (v)
4 **invest** (v)
5 **own** (v)
6 **personalize** (v)
7 **promise** (v)
8 **report** (v)

a to share thoughts, feelings, or information by speaking or writing

b to put money into a company or property in order to make more money

c to make or change something so that it is suitable for a particular person

d to try to persuade people to buy a product or service by announcing it on television, on the Internet, in newspapers, etc.

e to tell someone you will definitely do something

f to give a spoken or written summary of something

g to pay someone to do work for you

h to have an item or possession

2 Complete the sentences with words from Exercise 1 in the correct form.

1 It's important for companies to provide opportunities for customers to _____ by phone or by e-mail.

2 Very successful companies do not need to _____ because everyone already knows their brand.

3 It's important for companies to _____ their money in improving their products.

4 Customers want businesses to _____ their service. They want to be treated like a valued individual.

5 The best companies _____ the best people to work for them.

6 When a company _____ a successful brand, it becomes more valuable.

7 It's important for companies to _____ to their staff how well they are doing.

8 Businesses should not _____ customers a service they may not be able to deliver.

3 Check (✓) the sentences you think are true in Exercise 2. Compare your list with a partner and discuss why you think each statement is or is not true.

I think sentence one is true because …

Academic words

1 Match the words in bold with the correct definitions.

1 **concept** (n)
2 **constant** (adj)
3 **economic** (adj)
4 **initial** (adj)
5 **investment** (n)
6 **maintain** (v)
7 **priority** (n)
8 **unique** (adj)

a continuous or regular over a long period of time
b happening at the beginning of a process
c relating to trade or money, usually in business
d money used in a way that may earn you more money
e to make something stay the same
f not the same as anything or anyone else
g something important that must be done first or needs more attention than anything else
h an idea for something new

2 Complete the sentences with words from Exercise 1.

1 A _____ business model will always be successful because there is nothing else like it.
2 Businesses find it hard to keep up with _____ changes in technology.
3 Most businesses make decisions for financial or _____ reasons.
4 He thought of the _____ and then employed people to create the product.
5 One _____ for companies should be to keep customers happy.
6 It's important to make the _____ effort for a company to be successful later.
7 The company needs _____ to grow. We don't have enough money at the moment.
8 It is important to _____ interest in what you do as a job.

3 Discuss these questions with a partner.

1 Do you have any ideas for a unique business concept?
   One idea I have is …
   I think it is a unique concept because …
2 How could you get investment in the project?
   To get investment in the project I would …
   Another possibility would be to …

Writing model

You are going to use modals of obligation and necessity to write an essay introduction that answers the question about the most important parts of a successful business.

A Analyze

Read the model essay question and the brainstorm. Use the brainstorm to complete the introduction for the essay.

Do you agree that investing in new technology is the most important part of a successful business?

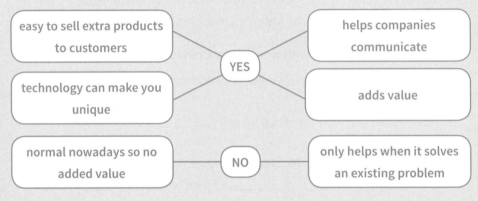

- easy to sell extra products to customers
- technology can make you unique

YES

- helps companies communicate
- adds value

- normal nowadays so no added value

NO

- only helps when it solves an existing problem

B Model

Every year, thousands of new companies appear. Investing in technology is likely to make them more successful. Technology does not have to be expensive, but maintaining investment in it can help companies [1]_____. It can also solve a number of issues for customers, personalize a business's services, and make a company [2]_____ and different to its competitors. This essay will first look at how technology must be a priority for small businesses and how it must solve existing [3]_____.

1 What is the main reason the writer thinks technology is important in a successful business?

    1 Technology helps companies to communicate and solves existing issues.

    2 Not all companies use technology well so it is an opportunity.

    3 New technology is expensive and therefore likely to result in success.

2 Discuss these questions with a partner.

    1 Do you agree that technology makes a company successful?

    2 Do you think these things add more or less value than technology?

          brand   good design   quality products

Grammar

Modals of obligation and necessity

Must, *need to*, and *have to* show there is a strong obligation to do something.

Form	Examples
subject + *must* + base form	*Businesses know that they **must** provide good customer service.*
subject + *need to* / *have to* + base form	*You **need to** think about the things customers value.*

Mustn't shows there is a strong obligation not to do something.

Don't have to and *don't need to* show that it isn't necessary to do something.

Form	Examples
subject + *mustn't* + base form	*Companies **mustn't** ignore their customers.*
subject + *don't have* / *don't need* + *to* + base form	*Companies **don't need to** spend as much on advertising.*

1 Choose the correct option to complete the sentences.

1 Companies **need / must** to deal with complaints quickly or they will lose customers.

2 Companies **have to / mustn't** invest in technology to communicate with customers online.

3 Expensive products **don't need to / must** be good quality for people to buy them.

4 Companies **need / don't have** to look after existing customers carefully because it is expensive to get new customers.

5 Some companies **mustn't / don't need to** invest in technology because their customers like traditional products.

2 Complete the sentences with the correct form of the modals and verbs in parentheses.

1 We _____ (**need / advertise**) more. No one knows our products.

2 Companies _____ (**must / promise**) customers products they cannot build.

3 She _____ (**have / wear**) a uniform for work. She wears her own clothes.

4 People _____ (**need / use**) travel agents anymore because everything can be booked online.

5 You _____ (**have / have**) a unique business idea. You can make an old idea better.

6 We _____ (**must / maintain**) excellence in our customer service or people will complain.

7 Start-ups _____ (**have / spend**) their money carefully or they will run out of money.

8 Companies _____ (**need / communicate**) with customers and e-mail them regularly.

3 Rewrite the sentences with the correct form of *mustn't, must, have to, don't have to, need to,* or *don't need to.* Sometimes more than one option is possible.

1 It's not important for him to invest in good offices.
   He _____.

2 I think it's necessary that she complains online.
   She _____.

3 It would be a really bad idea to delete that e-mail.
   You _____.

4 They are not worried about how expensive it is.
   They _____.

5 It's terrible when companies take a long time to answer the phone.
   Companies _____.

6 It's very important that schools have a website that is easy to use.
   Schools _____.

Writing skill

Writing an introduction

A good introduction needs to get the reader's interest. It needs to clearly and directly answer the essay question. For opinion essays, the introduction also needs to include your opinion. Lastly, it should signpost what the essay will cover. We often use phrases such as *"This essay will argue / look at / discuss …"* to signpost essays.

1   Look at these statements. Which two communicate the writer's opinion clearly?

   1   For the food industry, new technologies have both advantages and disadvantages.

   2   New technologies are allowing companies to meet their customers' needs.

   3   Customer service can be improved by investing in new technologies.

2   Read the *Writing an introduction* box. Which introduction do you think is better? Why?

   Essay question: Do you agree that customer service is the most important part of a successful restaurant business?

   ## Introduction A
   There are many priorities in the successful business model of a restaurant. Restaurants need to invest in quality food and develop a unique concept, but most importantly they must employ the right people to offer excellent customer service. This essay will first look at other factors that make a restaurant successful before arguing that good customer service must be the main priority.

   ## Introduction B
   Opening a new restaurant is one of the most popular start-ups. This is one of the main reasons why so many new companies fail, because the owners do not understand the main issues in the industry. This essay will argue that a better understanding of these issues, such as the importance of good customer service, would make more restaurants successful.

3   Put the sentences into the best order to form an introduction.

   A   A good brand means you can advertise clearly and communicate your ideas simply through the use of a logo. ___

   B   This essay will discuss what companies need to be successful and will then focus on why having a strong brand is the best way to add economic value. ___

   C   Brands are so important to the success of a company that many are worth billions of dollars. ___

Writing task

You are going to use modals of obligation and necessity to write an essay introduction that answers the question:

"Customer service is the most important part of a successful business. To what extent do you agree or disagree?"

Brainstorm

Complete the brainstorm below with ideas about what makes a business successful and adds value.

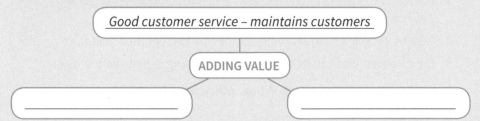

Plan

1 Do you think customer service is the most important part of a successful business? If not, what other things are more important?

2 If you think it is the most important part of a successful business, what reasons can you think of?

Write

Write an introduction to the essay question above. Remember to attract the reader's interest, answer the question specifically and outline the essay structure. Remember to use modals of obligation and necessity in your introduction. Your text should be 50 to 100 words long.

Share

Exchange paragraphs with a partner. Look at the checklist on page 189 and provide feedback on the structure of the introduction to your partner.

Rewrite and edit

Read your partner's comments. What could you change to make your writing better? Revise your text, then check it for errors. Think about:

• answering the question and your main opinion

• the signposting of what will be included in the essay.

Write the final draft.

Review

Wordlist

MACMILLAN
DICTIONARY

Vocabulary preview

access (n) ***	excellence (n) *	start-up (n)
adapt (v) **	existing (adj) ***	trust (v) ***
brand (n) **	logo (n) *	value (n) ***
business model (n) ***	make decisions	
customer service (n)	(phrase) ***	
entrepreneur (n)	quality (n) ***	

Vocabulary development

advertise (v) **	employ (v) ***	own (v) ***	promise (v) ***
communicate (v) **	invest (v) ***	personalize (v)	report (v) ***

Academic words

concept (n) ***	economic (adj) ***	investment (n) ***	priority (n) ***
constant (adj) ***	initial (adj) ***	maintain (v) ***	unique (adj) ***

Academic words review

Complete the sentences with the words in the box.

approach	concept	economic	priority	unique

1 This machine is more efficient and better designed than anything else on the market. It really is _____.

2 There are many things to do today, so we must decide what our number one _____ is.

3 Driverless cars are a new _____ and not everyone likes the idea!

4 Rising demand for goods and services is an important factor in a country's _____ growth.

5 There are many different ways to _____ a research project.

Unit review

Reading 1		I can identify supporting details in a text.
Reading 2		I can use signposting to navigate a text.
Study skill		I can identify soft skills that recruiters are looking for.
Vocabulary		I can use a range of verbs to discuss business.
Grammar		I can use modals of obligations and necessity.
Writing		I can write an essay introduction.

Discussion point

Discuss with a partner.

1 Look at the infographic. Did the family increase spending on objects or experiences?

2 Do you spend more on experiences or objects?

3 Do you agree that spending more on experiences makes people happier? Why / why not?

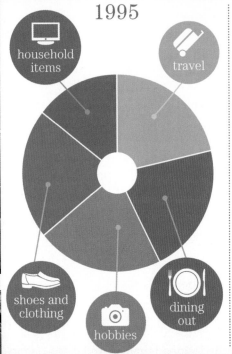
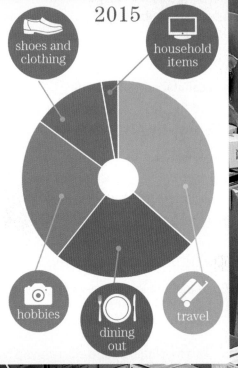

A family's spending

1995

household items

travel

shoes and clothing

hobbies

dining out

2015

shoes and clothing

household items

hobbies

dining out

travel

VIDEO

A "HANDY" WAY TO SHOP

Before you watch

Answer the questions with a partner.

1 How do you spend most of your money?

  A bank transfer

  B cash

  C check

  D card (using your pin)

  E contactless payment

2 Do you worry about the security of paying? Why / why not?

UNIT AIMS

READING 1 Understanding data
READING 2 Recognizing academic texts
STUDY SKILL Using tables, charts, and graphs

VOCABULARY Comparing and contrasting
GRAMMAR Simple past: irregular verbs
WRITING Summarizing trends in graphs

Workers in a busy Amazon warehouse.

While you watch

Read the sentences and then watch the video.
Choose the correct option to complete the sentences.

1 The slowest part of shopping was **choosing / paying**.

2 The technology scans **your finger / your hand**.

3 The system is secure because **it links to your tax number / everyone's hands are different**.

4 The students think it **is / isn't** safe.

After you watch

Answer the questions with a partner.

1 Do you think this system would be popular in your country?

   No, in my country …   Yes, I do, because …

2 What method of paying is most common in your country? Why do people prefer it?

   The most common way is … People prefer it because …

3 Do you think technology will completely replace shop assistants? Why / why not?

   Yes, I do, because …   No, I don't because …

The superconsumer generation

A Vocabulary preview

1 Complete the sentences with the words in the box.

| advertising consumer decade demand importance |
| multinational company power store |

1 Which companies have great _____ teams who promote products well?

2 Do you think large companies have too much _____ and control?

3 How often do you buy clothes in a _____ and how often do you buy them online?

4 Do you prefer small local stores or a big _____?

5 Do companies know the _____ of young customers today?

6 Think about the last _____. What things were popular then that are not popular now?

7 Is the _____ who buys the products the most important person for a business?

8 What products do young people want and _____ more of than older people?

2 Discuss the questions from Exercise 1 with a partner.

B Before you read

Preparing to read

Discuss these questions with a partner.

1 Where do you shop most often? Do you shop in different places to other people in your family?

I normally shop in … I buy / don't buy … online …

2 What was the last thing you bought from a store?

C Global reading

Understanding main ideas

Match the headings with paragraphs 2–6 of *The superconsumer generation*.

The growth of online sales

The growth of large stores

Generation Y's future importance

What is Generation Y?

Generation Y is hard to influence

The superconsumer generation

1 <u>*A mall for a new generation of consumers*</u>

At over a million square meters, and with over 1,200 stores, the Dubai Mall is huge in mall terms. The 750,000 people who visit it every week can find almost any product that meets their demands. Such mega-malls could be seen as a natural home for Generation Y, the biggest-spending and most demanding generation of consumers the world has ever seen.

2 _____

Generation Y is the name given to the group of people born between the late 1970s and mid-1990s. Their lives have happened at the same time as huge financial changes in the way we spend our money, and members of this group are demonstrating more and more financial behaviors across a range of countries and cultures.

3 _____

While their parents' generation knew many store owners personally when they were growing up, members of Generation Y are more likely to buy from huge multinational companies like Walmart. The biggest group of stores on the planet shows no signs of stopping. They grew from 8,500 stores in 15 countries in 2011 to over 11,500 stores in 28 different countries in 2015. That year Walmart made sales of just under 500 billion U.S. dollars, which is bigger than the GDP of 165 countries.

4 _____

While consumers of the Generation Y period can choose from a huge range of products at giant shopping malls, they have even more choice online. In just over a decade, Internet shopping saw huge growth. In the U.K., for example, consumers spent £800 million online in 2000; by 2015 this had grown to £114 billion. Amazon, the world's largest online store, sells such a wide variety of products they have to be kept in huge buildings the size of ten soccer fields.

5 _____

Gen Y-ers are the main target for many companies because of their spending power and attitude to shopping. In the U.S. alone, as a group they have $170 billion to spend and 31% earn enough money to live the life they choose. Unfortunately for companies, they are considered the hardest group to sell to. A large portion of Generation Y claim they are not influenced by advertising. Instead, one in three read blogs to seek suggestions and reviews before deciding what to buy. The group does not like to be influenced and are unlikely to believe any advertising message, but they do expect companies to personally interact with them on social media.

6 _____

The older and richer Gen Y consumers become, the more important it is for companies to understand them. If a company can use technology to personalize its products and services, it might just gain some of the richest technology-loving customers in history.

D Close reading

Texts often contain a range of data. Pay attention to prepositions around the numbers. These can tell you about the kinds of data in the text. For example:

between – suggests a period of time or a range of numbers

over / under – the number is not an exact amount

Also look for other symbols or words to indicate the type of data, such as currency signs ($ or £), percentages (%), or years (2010).

1 Read *The superconsumer generation* again. What do the following numbers refer to?

   1 A million square meters

   2 750,000

   3 15 and 28

   4 £800 million and £114 billion

   5 one in three

2 Read the text again. Write *T* (True), *F* (False), or *NG* (Not Given) for each sentence.

   1 Almost as many people go to the Dubai Mall every week as live in Dubai. ___

   2 Gen Y-ers were all born in the 1980s. ___

   3 People spend more on the Internet than in stores. ___

   4 31% percent of Generation Y-ers have enough money to live the lives they want. ___

   5 Gen Y-ers are not important consumers. ___

E Critical thinking

Discuss these questions in a group.

1 Think about how you shop and how your parents' and grandparents' generations shopped. Are they different from you?

   My grandparents / parents shop in … They usually / don't usually buy …

2 Do you think older generations are slower to use and like new technology for shopping than younger people? Why do you think so?

   They do / don't like new technology because …

Study skills | Using tables, charts, and graphs

Headings and labels help you to understand the data.

Headings: Read the main headings carefully. Note each word or phrase, and be sure you know exactly what the graph or table is meant to represent.

Labels: Read the labels on rows and columns axis and lines. These should tell you precisely what each represents.

Key: If color, shading or symbols are used, look for the key that explains these.

© Stella Cottrell (2013)

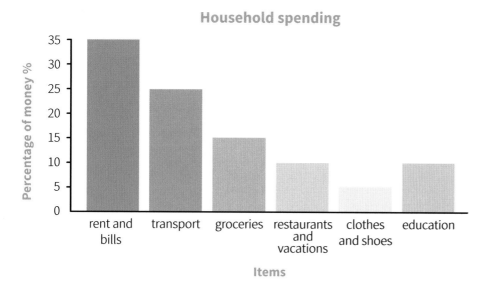

1 Read *Using tables, charts, and graphs* and look at the graph. Then:
- Underline the heading.
- Put a check symbol (✓) next to the horizontal axis.
- Circle next to the vertical axis.

2 Answer the questions about the bar chart.

1 What does the bar chart show?
  a Total amount of money households spend each month
  b Money households earn each month
  c Percentage of money spent on different items each month
2 Which three items did the household spend the most money on?
3 Which items did the household spend least on?

3 Do you think spending for households in your city is similar to the spending habits shown in the bar chart? Discuss your ideas with a partner.

Changing shopping habits

A Vocabulary preview

1 Complete the sentences with the words in the box.

| goods influence invention significant stream subject survey valuable |

1 There have been _____ changes to people's shopping habits in the last 20 years.

2 I often buy _____ online rather than in stores.

3 Fashion trends _____ what I buy. I love fashionable clothes.

4 People don't buy movies on DVD anymore. They _____ them.

5 I would answer a _____ to help stores find out about their customers.

6 I only buy cheap products online. I buy _____ things in store.

7 The cell phone is the most important _____ in the last 50 years.

8 I would be a good _____ for a study about shopping habits.

2 Check (✓) the sentences that are true for you in Exercise 1. Compare your opinions with a partner.

B Before you read

Recognizing academic texts

There are two main categories for academic texts: texts based on **primary research** and texts based on **secondary research**.

Primary research …

is **done by the writer** and usually shows method, results, discussion, and conclusion. For example, survey results and scientific studies.

Secondary research …

is **based on other people's research** and usually follows a basic essay structure: introduction, main body, conclusion. For example, opinion and discussion essays.

1 Look at the headings in *Changing shopping habits*. Is the text based on primary or secondary research?

2 How might the text be useful? Check (✓) all that are true.

1 ☐ As a source of theories

2 ☐ For statistics to provide examples of points you want to make

3 ☐ For quotes from experts in the field

4 ☐ To find data that explains a point you want to make

CHANGING
SHOPPING HABITS

1 INTRODUCTION

Since the start of the Internet in the early 1990s there has been an increase in online shopping. Some of the most well-known brands and biggest companies operate only online. The Internet has changed the way companies work and how customers shop like no other invention in the last 100 years. However, people also still love shopping in stores. This research paper will investigate shopping trends for 18- to 25-year-old male and female students in the key areas of vacations, food, clothing, and entertainment. The statistics from this survey show that there has been a significant growth in online sales in all areas apart from clothing.

2 METHOD

A survey was created and sent out online to students across three universities. The students were all aged 18 to 25, with an even split of men and women. Four groups of eight students were then selected to take part in focus groups to find out further information behind the reasons for their answers.

3 RESULTS
WHAT, HOW, AND WHY PEOPLE BUY ONLINE

The first section of the survey looked at people's general online shopping behavior. In total, 80% of those surveyed had shopped online in the last three months. The goods most often bought were clothes, food, electronics, health and beauty products, and entertainment products. As can be seen in Figure 1.1, many students had bought most items online at some point in a 12-month phase. Only clothing and beauty products were bought by under 50% of the students. While not bought frequently, vacations were actually booked only online by almost all students. The main reasons given for preferring online shopping were: cheaper prices for valuable items, no waiting in line, shopping 24 hours a day, easy to compare products, and cheap and quick home delivery. The method of shopping online is also gradually changing with more things bought on cell phones. The survey showed similar results for different genders, both male and female students.

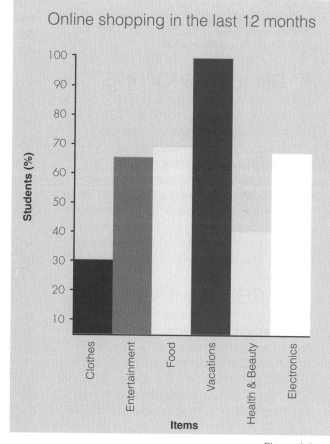

Figure 1.1

GLOSSARY

focus group (n) a small group of people who are interviewed together to help with research

4 VACATIONS

One big change in online shopping is how customers are using the Internet to buy vacations. Like many other categories, spending has increased a lot on vacations and travel and, for the subjects of this survey, it is now the only method used to book vacations. In addition, the way people use the Internet while traveling is changing as well. The survey found one in five of the students now blog while traveling. People trust vacation reviews from friends or family the most, followed by online reviews from other travelers. Over half of the subjects' vacation choice is influenced by friends' photos on social media. People are also much more likely (just under half) to change their mind after reading reviews on websites. The increasing influence of friends and online reviews means that very few people now buy vacations from travel agents.

5 GROCERY SHOPPING

A large number of the students, just under 70%, bought food online in the last 12 months. However, nearly all the students used both online shopping and in-store shopping for groceries. Many used online shopping for a large weekly shop. The main reasons for shopping online were ease and speed. One in three of the students now orders with next-day delivery. The reasons to shop in store were mainly to buy fresh fruit and vegetables and because they had run out of essential items.

6 ENTERTAINMENT

Another major change is in how people buy entertainment products. Clearly, the Internet is changing how quickly people demand products and services, as is demonstrated in Figure 1.2. Between 2014 and 2016, streaming and downloading of movies and TV programs overtook sales of online DVDs for the subjects of this survey. Online DVD sales are declining, but in-store DVD sales have nearly disappeared. Not only do the students demand physical products quickly, but there is also a growth in the demand for watching entertainment instantly.

7 CLOTHING

Clothing, along with health and beauty products, were found to be some of the least popular products bought online. The main reason given was the desire to try on clothes before buying them. Students wanted to see how the clothes looked before buying them, especially if they were valuable and expensive. Many felt that they returned clothes to online stores too often and that this made the whole process slower and more difficult.

8 DISCUSSION AND CONCLUSIONS

The results of this research highlight the growing trend to shop more online. Not only are people shopping more online but they are also being influenced by the online views of friends, bloggers, and reviewers. Speed and ease appear to be the main reasons for the increases in online shopping. However, these factors have not made people change their shopping habits for clothes and beauty products. In conclusion, improvements in technology are only likely to increase this trend in coming years.

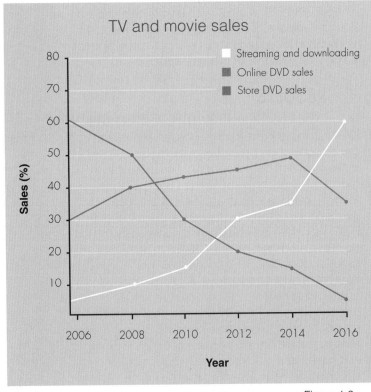

Figure 1.2

C Global reading

READING 2

Completing a summary

Read *Changing shopping habits* quickly and choose the correct words to complete the summary.

Online shopping is popular because of how [1] **quick / safe** and simple it is. People like to buy [2] **snacks / fresh food** and things they have run out of in stores. Streaming and downloads are more popular than physical [3] **books / DVDs**. Clothing and beauty items [4] **are / are not** popular to buy online, since items often need to be [5] **returned / delivered** to the stores.

D Close reading

Understanding charts and graphs

Look at the bar chart and line graph in the text. Complete the sentences with information from the graph and chart.

1 The bar chart shows the percentage of people who bought things online in the previous _____.

2 Nearly 100% of the students have bought _____ online.

3 Between 60 and _____ of the students have bought entertainment products, food, and electronics online.

4 The line graph shows the ten years between _____ and _____.

5 We cannot see total sales, but we can see the _____ of people buying with each method.

6 In-store DVD sales were under _____ in 2016.

7 Streaming and downloading is the highest at _____.

8 Streaming grew fastest between _____ and _____.

E Critical thinking

1 The survey mentions trends in sales of vacations, entertainment, food, and clothes. Which trends are most similar in your country?

The trend most similar to my country is …

2 The survey only looked at students aged 18–25. How does this influence the research? Think about differences between countries, the number of people in a study, and the number of people in each country.

The age group influences the research because …

The number of people is significant because …

Vocabulary development

Comparing and contrasting

We use words for **comparing** to describe **similarities**, and words of **contrast** to describe **differences**.

1 Read the sentences and decide if the words in bold describe similarities or differences. Write *S* or *D*.

1 Paper book sales have fallen, **while** e-book sales have grown. ___

2 The dresses look **alike**, but one is more expensive than the other. ___

3 Almost **as many** shop in malls **as** shop online. ___

4 Online vacation prices **compared with** in-store ones are much cheaper. ___

5 They both sell an **equal** number of books. ___

6 Many big stores and companies **have** a lot **in common**. ___

7 You can see **the difference between** the more expensive laptop and the cheaper one. ___

2 Choose the best words from Exercise 1 to complete the sentences.

1 People used to buy vacations in stores _____ today most people book online.

2 _____ two generations is often shown through music, fashion, and business.

3 _____ previous generations, who saved to buy goods, many people now use credit cards.

4 Older generations _____ much more _____ with younger generations than they think.

5 The prices in store are _____ to those online.

6 All stores are _____ today because multinational companies are everywhere.

3 Discuss these questions with a partner using words for comparing and contrasting.

1 Do you shop in a similar or different way to your friends?

2 What are the main differences between shopping online and in stores?

3 What's the difference between how you spend your money now compared with five years ago?

Academic words

1 Match the words in bold with the correct definitions.

1	**decline** (v)	a	to become less or worse
2	**demonstrate** (v)	b	a part of an amount or total
3	**financial** (adj)	c	to show clearly that something is true or exists
4	**gender** (n)	d	a particular period of time, usually during the development of something
5	**phase** (n)		
6	**portion** (n)	e	to ask for something or try to find something
7	**seek** (v)	f	involving money
8	**target** (n)	g	something that you try to achieve or an audience you want
		h	the state of being male or female

2 Complete the sentences with words from Exercise 1.

1 The first _____ of the research involved sending out a survey to 1,000 people.

2 People under 40 spend a large _____ of their money online.

3 _____ does not influence online spending much. In most areas men and women spend the same.

4 We made the money we needed to achieve our _____.

5 I like to see someone _____ a new computer before I buy one so I know how it works.

6 There was a 20% _____ from 10,000 to 8,000 in the last month.

7 She decided to _____ the opinion of her friends to find out what they thought.

8 Most new businesses fail because of _____ reasons.

3 Tell your partner about:

1 A product you shop for regularly. Who is the target audience?

2 A product whose sales you think are declining. Why?

Writing model

You are going to learn to use simple past irregular verbs to write a summary of past trends in a graph.

Look at the line graph below showing food trends with four products. Describe and compare the data. Write no more than 150 words.

A Analyze

Look at the line graph and complete the description.

The graph shows the average [1]_____ per person. It focuses on four foods / drink: organic food, bread, [2]_____, and [3]_____. The vertical axis shows the grams / milliliters eaten each [4]_____. The horizontal axis shows the [5]_____.

B Model

Average food consumption

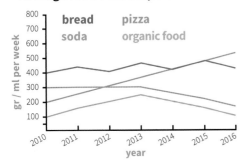

[1] The graph demonstrates the changes in average food consumption between 2010 and 2016. [2] In general, the amount of pizza consumed increased significantly while the amount of soda drunk declined. [3] While the amount of pizza eaten increased steadily over the whole period, the amount of soda drunk remained stable for 3 years and then declined between 2013 and 2016. [4] There was little change in the quantity of bread and organic food eaten over the whole period. [5] The main difference was that the amount of organic food rose slowly between 2010 and 2013 before falling again to the original level, whereas the quantity of bread rose and fell over the whole period. [6] Overall, while the amount of organic food and bread consumed remained about the same over the period, the amount of pizza eaten increased significantly and the amount of soda drunk decreased.

1   Read the summary and answer these questions.

   1   Which sentence introduces the graph?

   2   Which sentences explain the main features?

   3   Which sentence summarizes what the graph shows?

2   Look at the foods and drinks below. Do you think people eat and drink more, less, or the same amount for each one compared to 15 years ago?

| burgers   chocolate   coffee   dairy products |
| fresh fruit   meat   microwave meals   vegetables |

3   Compare your ideas with a partner. Give reasons for your decisions.

   I think burger sales have definitely increased because we have a lot more fast food restaurants.

Grammar

Simple past: irregular verbs

We use the simple past to talk about: a specific, completed past action, a series of completed past actions, past actions over a period of time, and habits or repeated past actions.

Regular verbs follow a pattern:

Affirmative	Negative
subject + base form of verb + *-ed* *Sales increased.*	subject + *did not (didn't)* + base form of verb *Sales didn't increase.*

Irregular verbs do not follow a pattern:

rise → **rose**   fall → **fell**   sell → **sold**

*Many **felt** that they returned clothes to online stores too often.*

Prepositions can be used with some irregular verbs to show the difference between two points.

*Their target fell **from** $200 **to** just under $150.*

*People spent more on pizza **between** 2005 and 2010.*

1   Work with a partner. Match the sentences with the correct use of the simple past.

1   I bought a coffee every day last week. ___   a   a series of past actions
2   Cell phone sales grew between 2012 and 2017. ___   b   past actions over a period of time
3   He left the house and drove to the mall. ___   c   repeated past action
4   She lost her bag yesterday. ___   d   completed past action

2 Complete the sentences with the simple past form of the verbs in parentheses.

1 More people _____ (choose) to stream their favorite movies last year than go to the cinema.

2 Access to movies online _____ (cost) a lot more in the past.

3 The company _____ (sell) more products online than in store.

4 According to the chart, sales _____ (rise); they stayed the same.

5 Sales _____ (grow) last year. They _____ (fall) for the first time in five years.

6 He _____ (send) back the clothes he bought online.

7 The company _____ (begin) with just one store in 1980.

8 I didn't order a new card because I _____ (find) my old one.

9 I _____ (feel) the shoes were too expensive.

10 What _____ (be) the last thing you _____ (buy)?

3 Complete the sentences with *by, to, from, between* and the simple past form of the verbs in parentheses.

1 Sales _____ (grow) _____ 10%.

2 Online shopping _____ (rise) quickly _____ 2012 and 2017.

3 The number of customers per day _____ (increase) _____ 500 last year _____ 750 today.

4 Work with a partner. What was the last gift you bought? Who was it for? How did you choose what to get?

Writing skill

Start with a sentence describing what the graph shows. It is then important to describe the biggest changes and give a summary sentence about the main trends in the graph.

We use a range of words to describe changes in graphs.

Verbs: *rose, fell, increased, decreased, remained*

Adverbs: *quickly, gradually, slightly, significantly, dramatically, steadily*

Nouns: *increase, fall*

Adjectives: *small, significant, slight, dramatic, steady*

1 Look at the line graph. Choose the best description of what the graph shows.

    a The graph shows changes in how a class of students bought books between 2005 and 2015.

    b The graph shows the changes in books between 2005 and 2015.

    c The graph shows changes of three different lines between 2005 and 2015.

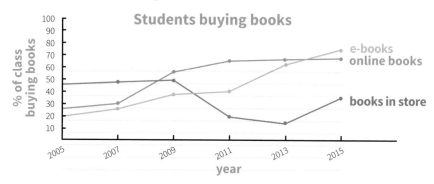

2 Look at the graph and complete the sentences with the words in the box.

    dramatically   fell   gradually   grew   increase   sharply   steady

Buying books in store remained quite [1]_____ between 2005 and 2009. It [2]_____ quickly between 2009 and 2011. Buying books in store began to [3]_____ in 2013.

Buying books online increased [4]_____ between 2007 and 2009. It then grew [5]_____.

The portion of the class buying e-books [6]_____ steadily until 2011, when it increased [7]_____.

3 Complete the sentence showing an overview of the main trends.

Overall the graph shows that [1]_____ became less popular and then started to increase, while sales of books online and [2]_____ continued to grow.

Writing task

You're going to write a summary of past trends in a graph.

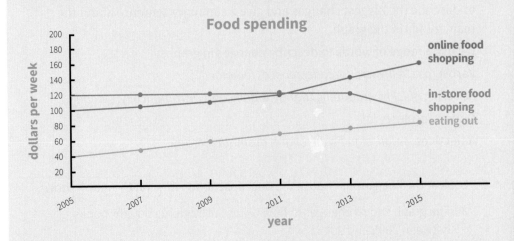

Food spending

Brainstorm

Look at the graph and make a note of the most important changes and trends.

Plan

Answer the following questions as you plan your description.

1 List three of the main changes.
2 In general, what does the graph show about what we spend on food?

Write

Using your answers to the questions above, write a description of the graph. Use words to describe change. Pay attention to your use of the simple past and irregular verbs. Your text should be about 150 words long.

Share

Exchange paragraphs with a partner. Look at the checklist on page 189 and provide feedback to your partner.

Rewrite and edit

Read your partner's comments. What could you change to make your writing better? Revise your text, then check it for errors. Think about:

- simple past verb forms

- summarizing and highlighting key information only.

Write the final draft.

Review

Wordlist

MACMILLAN
DICTIONARY

Vocabulary preview

advertising (n) **	goods (n pl) ***	multinational company (n)	stream (v) *
consumer (n) ***	importance (n) ***		subject (n) ***
decade (n) ***	influence (v) ***	power (n) ***	survey (n) ***
demand (v) ***	invention (n) **	significant (adj) ***	valuable (adj) ***
		store (n) ***	

Vocabulary development

alike (adv) *	equal (adj) ***	the difference between (phrase)	while (conj) ***
as many … as … (phrase)	have (a lot) in common (phrase)		
compared with (phrase)			

Academic words

decline (v) ***	financial (adj) ***	phase (n) ***	seek (v) ***
demonstrate (v) ***	gender (n) **	portion (n) **	target (n) ***

Academic words review

Complete the sentences with the words in the box.

demonstrate	domestic	financial	maintain	phases

1 GDP stands for Gross _____ Product. It refers to the monetary value of the finished goods and services a country produces in a year.

2 The company needs to borrow more money again. Its _____ situation is getting worse and worse.

3 There are five _____ in the company's expansion plan. First of all, we will build a new factory in China.

4 It is very important to _____ your audience's interest when giving a presentation.

5 "This is the latest kind of coffee machine. Would you like me to _____ it for you?"

Unit review

Reading 1	☐	I can understand data in a text.
Reading 2	☐	I can recognize academic texts.
Study skill	☐	I can understand tables, charts, and graphs.
Vocabulary	☐	I can use words for comparing and contrasting.
Grammar	☐	I can use the simple past with irregular verbs.
Writing	☐	I can summarize trends in graphs.

Discussion point

Discuss with a partner.

1 Look at these quotations about success. Which do you agree with? Why?

*I agree with ...
because ...*

2 Which quotes talk about failure and success? Do you agree that you need to fail to be successful?

I think / don't think you need to fail to be successful because ...

3 What things do you think are a sign of success?

I think ... is a sign of success because ...

What is success?

"The most important single ingredient in the formula of success is knowing how to get along with people."
Theodore Roosevelt

"Success is dependent on effort."
Sophocles

"We are all failures – at least the best of us are."
J.M. Barrie

"Be patient, for the world is broad and wide."
William Shakespeare

"I have not failed. I've just found 10,000 ways that won't work."
Thomas A. Edison

VIDEO

KEEPING ACTIVE

Before you watch

Answer the questions with a partner.

1 What things are there for young people to do in your home town?
2 What things are there for old people to do in your home town?
3 How could your home town be improved for young and old people?

UNIT AIMS

READING 1 Pronoun reference
READING 2 Identifying reasons
STUDY SKILL Your vision of success as a student

VOCABULARY *re-* prefixes to describe change
GRAMMAR Determiners of quantity
WRITING Describing locations and changes

Fireworks at Victoria Harbor, Hong Kong.

While you watch

Check (✓) the sentences that are true in the video.

☐ There are not so many young people who use the playgrounds in Tokyo.

☐ Exercise helps Japanese people live longer.

☐ You need to be fit to do the classes.

After you watch

Answer the questions with a partner.

1 Do you think it's important to provide parks for older people?

   Yes, because …   *No, because …*

2 What type of exercise do older people do in your country?

   In my country they …

3 Is it important for a successful city to think about all of the people that live there?

   Yes, because …   *No, because …*

Failing to succeed

A Vocabulary preview

1 Complete the sentences with the words and phrases in the box.

| ability | attempt | believe in | deal with |
| failure | go wrong | opportunity | succeed |

1 I feel confident I will do well on this course. I _____ myself.

2 When I don't _____ I feel really bad. I only like doing things I know I will achieve.

3 When things _____ I feel embarrassed and don't want to see other people.

4 I think I will be successful in life; I just need the right _____. This chance will make me a success.

5 I _____ problems quickly so they no longer bother me.

6 I always edit and rewrite my essays. I never hand in the first _____.

7 I have the _____ to succeed at anything when I try hard.

8 I worry about _____ and not doing well. It stops me trying.

2 Check (✓) the sentences that are true for you. Compare your choices with a partner.

B Before you read

Preparing to read

Discuss these questions with a partner.

1 How do you and people you know feel when you experience failure?
   When I fail I feel embarrassed and annoyed.

2 Have you ever learned something from failure? What did you learn?
   I didn't hand an essay in on time, but I learned to manage my time better.

C Global reading

Understanding main ideas

Match the paragraph with the correct main argument.

Paragraph 2 ___   a How to react to failure

Paragraph 3 ___   b Changing our feelings about failure

Paragraph 4 ___   c The importance in believing in what you are doing

Paragraph 5 ___   d The importance of trying to continue

Failing to succeed

1 Many people fear failure and try to avoid it even when they have the opportunity to succeed. One way we protect how we value ourselves is by believing in our own ability and by convincing others of it as well. As a result, many people won't attempt something if they think they might fail. Altering our view so that failure is fine and nothing to worry about could be the key to opening opportunities to be successful in life.

2 Failure is an aspect of everyone's life. However, when we think of experiencing failure we shouldn't think of ourselves as a failure. People often feel ashamed or embarrassed when things go wrong, but failure actually gives us the chance to learn, adapt, and improve. When companies find that a product is unpopular and not doing well, they often take the opportunity to improve the product, and doing so can make them more successful as a business. People can also look at their own bad experiences as an opportunity to learn and improve. For example, if someone does badly in a job interview, they can learn what went wrong and do better in the next one. In fact, nearly winning can make people much more determined to succeed in the future. It gives us a feeling of nearly being successful and makes us much more determined to succeed next time we try.

3 Passion is also a vital part of being successful. When people constantly say no to your ideas, enjoying what you do can push you forward to continue. You are motivated to keep trying because you are doing it for yourself or something you believe in, like a charity. Some people connect success to ideas such as fame and making money. While these are ways to measure your success, there are also many other ways such as how happy your achievements make you. Feeling good because you are doing something you love or are supporting others, can be one way of viewing your own success, even when others don't recognize your achievements.

4 Not only do people need passion to succeed they also need to keep trying—the ability to not give up is essential. People can be intelligent, talented, or have a lot of common sense but because success takes time, sometimes people give up before they reach their goals. In some professions, such as working in movies, you need to quickly get used to people saying no. Steven Spielberg famously failed to get into college to study movies and was rejected more than once. He then went on to become one of the most successful movie directors of all time. Every failed attempt is difficult, but each one can make us stronger if we react in the right way. The ability to not give up and keep going is part of nearly all successful people's personalities.

5 Whether you want to be a writer, a business person, or a musician, being successful will mean you have to deal with a lot of failure. Lots of people see this as a lack of ability, but arguably it should just be seen as a step towards success.

GLOSSARY

passion (n) a strong interest in something

Using pronoun reference

D Close reading

Writers use pronoun reference to avoid repeating words, to add organization, and to help you understand how ideas are connected in a text. Simple pronoun referents include *he*, *she*, and *it*, *this*, *that*, *these*, and *those*. Other referents include *one*, e.g. *this one*, *that one*, *each one*, *the next one*. *One* usually refers to a noun in the text. Look at the words and sentences before and after the referent to understand what they refer to. For example:

The author's first book failed, but her second one was a success.

1   Find these phrases in *Failing to succeed*. What do each of the pronouns in bold refer to?

1   by convincing others of **it** (paragraph 1)

_____

2   do better in the next **one** (paragraph 2)

_____

3   While **these** are ways to measure your success (paragraph 2)

_____

4   **He** then went on to become (paragraph 4)

_____

5   each **one** can make us stronger (paragraph 4)

_____

2   Read *Failing to succeed* again and find the details used to support these points.

1   Bad experiences people can learn from
2   Why people who love what they do are motivated to succeed
3   Why people give up before they reach their goals
4   Jobs that take a long time to succeed in

E Critical thinking

1   The text says that people do not try because they are scared to fail. Do you agree with this? Why / why not?

I think / don't think this is true because …

2   What do you remember from the text? When can failure make us successful? Can you think of examples that are not in the text?

Failure can help us by …

Study skills | Your vision of success as a student

Students invest a great deal of time, energy and money in their Higher Education so success at university or at college is usually very important to them. However, there are many different versions of what that success would look like.

The way you spend your time as a student is key to whether you achieve what you really want from the experience. It is largely up to you to decide how you do that. If you can formulate a clearer vision of what success as a student means to you, you are more likely to achieve it.

© Stella Cottrell (2013)

1 Match the different scenarios with the type of success.

1 I passed my driving test at the first attempt. ___
2 I won the local tennis tournament. ___
3 I got the grades I needed to get into a good college. ___
4 I saved money to buy a new laptop. ___

a academic success
b personal success
c sporting success
d financial success

2 Think about your own academic, personal, sporting, and financial achievements and tell a partner about them. What difficulties did you have when trying to achieve these things?

3 Read *Your vision of success as a student*. Write one sentence that describes what being a successful student means to you.

_____

4 Write down your personal goals for studying. What can you do with your time at college to help you achieve these goals?

Goals	What I can do
_____	_____
_____	_____
_____	_____

Building a success

A Vocabulary preview

1 Match the words in bold with the correct definitions.

1	**demolish** (v)	a	plants and animals
2	**employment** (n)	b	to destroy or knock down
3	**former** (adj)	c	a grassy area such as a park or field
4	**green space** (n)	d	describing something that was true in the past
5	**income** (n)	e	a job or a situation where you are paid to work
6	**run-down** (adj)	f	to make someone or something completely different, usually to improve
7	**transform** (v)		
8	**wildlife** (n)	g	in bad condition due to no investment
		h	wages or money that someone receives

2 Complete the sentences with words from Exercise 1.

1 When organizations _____ one part of a city to be very different, it helps many other parts of the city.

2 You can only be successful if you have a good _____.

3 Cities should _____ ugly buildings and build new ones.

4 Every area needs to have a _____ for children to play in.

5 _____ factories should be changed to give them a new use such as a museum or gallery.

6 When an area is _____ and not nice to live in, crime will increase.

7 _____ in cities needs to be looked after, especially rare animals or plants.

8 People often move to places where they can find _____.

3 Check (✓) the opinions you agree with in Exercise 2. Compare with a partner.

B Before you read

Predicting

Look at the heading and pictures in the text. What changes do you think are described in the text?

C Global reading

1 Skim *Building a success* and check your predictions from *B Before you read*.

Identifying opinions

2 Read the text again and decide if these places in New York are considered successful, unsuccessful, or both successful and unsuccessful today.

1 High Line   2 Brooklyn   3 Fort Greene

Building a
SUCCESS

1 Many areas of cities that were once run-down are now successful and beautiful places. Investment and the right ideas transform these places and make them exciting places to live. One city to have been transformed is the American city of New York. The city was not considered a particularly nice place in the 1970s and some parts were in a particularly poor condition. As a result, there has been investment in the development of a number of areas. The city is now one of the best places to live in America.

2 A lot of neighborhoods, including large parts of Brooklyn, were once full of crime but are now safe and popular. The business areas of Flatiron and the Garment District now have new restaurants opening almost every week. Even a former train line, the High Line, was transformed into a beautiful green space with wildlife throughout. New York is a city that is always developing and improving and a good example of a modern and successful city.

3 In 1934 the High Line opened to trains taking goods to and from Manhattan's largest industrial area. However, as transportation moved to roads, the line became less and less used. As a result, it closed in 1980. While not being used, the area slowly became less attractive. Some people wanted to demolish the line while Peter Obletz, a local resident, decided to try to stop it being destroyed. In 1999 an organization called "Friends of the High Line" was started by Joshua David and Robert Hammond. Their motivation was to protect the High Line and reuse it as an outdoor public space. They decided to change it into a beautiful green, open space for the public to use.

GLOSSARY

industrial (adj) describes an area with many industries, often related to making things

4 The High Line is now a beautiful open park. The design chosen is based on the plants that grew on the out-of-use tracks. Changing each section of the High Line from an out-of-use train line to a green space involved years of planning and ideas from the community. Some of the city's most creative designers worked on the project and each section took a long time to complete. The last section of the park, the High Line at the Rail Yards, finally opened in 2014. In total, it took 15 years of effort to preserve the whole thing. Today the park gets nearly five million visitors every year and the value of property in the area has increased a lot.

5 It's not just New York's parks and transportation that have changed, but its boroughs have too. One area of the city that has transformed in the last decade is Brooklyn. The area once had high levels of crime and poverty. Now it is considered an attractive place to go to. An increasing number of students have started to attend the local schools and many trendy stores and restaurants have opened up. The number of tech start-ups opening in the area has also grown quickly. The once run-down area has completely changed. Due to the schools and job opportunities, many believe Brooklyn's changes to be a success and the care and maintenance given to its features make it an attractive place to live.

6 While the changes have mainly been positive, some people do not see it this way. Fort Greene, a neighborhood in the north-western part of Brooklyn, was originally a shipbuilding area. The area suffered from unemployment and crime for a long time because the shipping industry closed in the late 1960s. In 2004 the government decided to develop the area. Since then, it has changed a lot with the creation of new, luxury, high-rise buildings. However, since local people cannot pay the higher rents in this popular place they have had to move out. It also means there is less space for small businesses as national stores have transferred their offices to the area.

7 There are a number of ideas to try to stop this and make the changes work for everyone. On account of the expensive rents, all new projects to build accommodation must make places available for people with lower incomes. The city also plans to build new schools and community centers and to improve parks in these areas. Not everyone believes it will work but, if it does in one area of East New York, then there are plans to use it as a model across other parts of the city.

8 Over time, cities change, start showing signs of age, and begin to look run-down. Projects to improve these areas are important to the success of a city because they help the economy, reduce crime, and help make people feel proud of where they live. However, it is important that changes work for everybody as success means different things to different people.

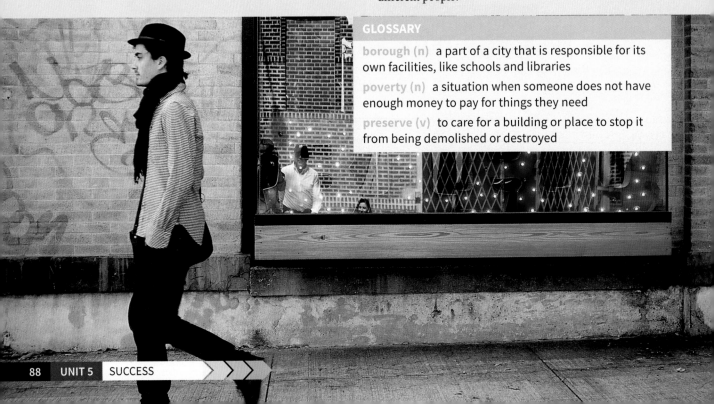

GLOSSARY

borough (n) a part of a city that is responsible for its own facilities, like schools and libraries

poverty (n) a situation when someone does not have enough money to pay for things they need

preserve (v) to care for a building or place to stop it from being demolished or destroyed

D Close reading

> Reasons for an event or situation are often given in a text to explain or support a main idea. It is important to identify these as they will give you an understanding of why something occurs. There are certain phrases that highlight reasons, for example:
>
> *because, due to, since, on account of, based on, as a result, the reason why.*

1 Scan the text and answer the questions.

1 Why did the High Line train close?

a It was too expensive. b It wasn't used enough.

2 Why was the current design for the High Line chosen?

a Plants already grew there. b The local people voted.

3 Why do many see the changes in Brooklyn as a success?

a There are more schools and job opportunities. b New cafés opened.

4 Why did crime increase in Fort Greene?

a An important industry closed. b The government did not invest enough.

5 Why have local people moved out of the area?

a There is not enough employment. b Rents have become too high.

6 Why must new building projects include accommodation with cheap rents?

a Some parts are now too expensive. b Not enough people want to live there.

2 Write the phrase used to introduce each reason (1–6) in Exercise 1.

3 Read *Building a success* again. Write *T* (True), *F* (False), or *NG* (Not Given) for each sentence.

1 New York was a nice place to live in the 1970s. ___
2 The High Line opened in 1934. ___
3 Nine people worked for Friends of the High Line when it started. ___
4 It took 20 years to preserve the High Line. ___
5 The Fort Greene shipping industry closed in the 1960s. ___

E Critical thinking

1 Think about the changes to Brooklyn described in *Building a success*. Do you think the changes made the area successful? Why / why not?

2 Answer the questions in groups.

1 Think of an area of your home town. How would you change it?
2 Would everyone like the changes? Who would and who wouldn't?

Vocabulary development

Describing change with *re-* prefixes

1 Match the actions with the objects.

1	**react** (v)	a	a failed test
2	**rearrange** (v)	b	old newspapers
3	**rebuild** (v)	c	a membership for another year
4	**recycle** (v)	d	an old car with a new car
5	**redo** (v)	e	things to put them in new locations
6	**renew** (v)	f	an old water bottle by filling it with tap water
7	**replace** (v)	g	to a problem
8	**reuse** (v)	h	something that has fallen down

2 Complete the sentences with actions from Exercise 1.

1 The designers tried to _____ the location of things in the park to improve it.

2 They want to _____ the old factory with a new school.

3 People might _____ positively to the changes and think they're successful.

4 I'm really pleased. My company is going to _____ my contract. I have another year's work.

5 They are planning to _____ the houses that were destroyed in the earthquake.

6 I _____ all the plastic, paper, and card I use.

7 I'm not happy with the report. Can you _____ it, please?

8 If people _____ plastic carrier bags and bottles there will be less waste in the park.

3 Write down something you usually *reuse*, *recycle*, *rearrange*, *renew*, and *redo*. Tell your partner about the things and why you do each one.

Academic words

1 Match the words in bold with the correct definitions.

1	**alter** (v)	a	the people who live in an area
2	**aspect** (n)	b	an important part of something that people usually notice
3	**community** (n)		
4	**feature** (n)	c	a feeling of enthusiasm or interest that makes you determined to do something
5	**maintenance** (n)		
6	**motivation** (n)	d	to turn away or not accept
7	**reject** (v)	e	to make something different
8	**transfer** (v)	f	work that is done to keep something in a good condition
		g	to move someone or something from one place to another
		h	a particular part of something

2 Complete the sentences with words from Exercise 1 in the correct form.

1 A good boss gives their team the _____ to succeed.

2 Often people only need to _____ something slightly to be successful.

3 People often need to _____ from one company to another to earn more money.

4 One of the most important _____ of success is hard work.

5 We need to look after the popular and important _____ of the city.

6 A poor _____ often just needs support in order to be successful.

7 Lots of successful people are _____. The important thing is then how you react.

8 For a city to be a nice place to live, the buildings must have regular _____.

3 What aspects of a good community make it successful? Complete the sentences with your ideas.

1 The facilities are important because _____
_____.

2 It's vital to have the right location because _____
_____.

3 Transportation links make a community successful because they _____
_____.

4 Having the right business helps because people need _____
_____.

Writing model

You are going to learn about determiners of quantity and how to describe locations and changes in order to describe improvements to a place as shown on two plans.

The two maps show a park in 2010 and 2015. Summarize the information by selecting and reporting the main features, and make relevant comparisons.

2010   2015

A Model

Read the model answer and circle words that describe change.

The two maps show the changes to a park between 2010 and 2015. In 2010, the park was mostly polluted and unused and there was too much garbage that needed to be removed. The run-down area was transformed into a much nicer park in 2015. A lot of the buildings changed, with the former gas station replaced by a children's education center. To the south of this, the old factory was renewed as a factory museum with a café. Too much of the area was polluted or unused and these aspects were cleaned up. The old train line in the middle of the park was replaced with a nature walk and a few trees in the same location. To the northeast the polluted lake became a boating lake. To the south of this, the garbage was removed and a new playground feature was added.

B Analyze

Look at the diagram and read the model answer. Then answer the questions.

1 What were the main changes?

2 How do you think the area improved?

3 Why would a town or city want to renovate an area like this?

4 Why do you think the area became popular with residents in 2015?

Grammar

Determiners of quantity

Determiners of quantity are used to show how much or how little there is of something.

> *A large amount*
> There was **a lot of** crime in the area.
> **A few** tennis courts were built.
> **Very few** businesses opened.
> Twenty years ago, there were **hardly any** coffee shops.
> In 2006, there were **no** bridges in the town.
> *None*

Use **much** in questions and negatives with non-count nouns. **Much** is used to mean a large quantity or to ask about a large quantity. Use **a lot of** with non-count nouns in positive sentences.	There isn't **much** garbage in the area. Was there **much** garbage in the area? There was **a lot of** garbage in the area.
Use **many** in positives, negatives, and questions with count nouns.	There were **many** run-down buildings in the area. There aren't **many** run-down buildings. How **many** run-down buildings are there?
Add **too** when there is a lot of something and it is negative.	There was **too much** trash in the park. There are **too many** cars on the roads.

1 Complete the sentences with *wasn't much* or *weren't many*.

1 There _____ parks in my city when I was younger.

2 There _____ unemployment in my city.

3 There _____ factories on the edge of the city.

4 There _____ pollution in my city.

2 Make the sentences in Exercise 1 positive.

1 _____

2 _____

3 _____

4 _____

3 Which sentences are correct? Check (✓) the correct sentences.

1 ☐ Downtown didn't have much green space.

2 ☐ There is much wildlife downtown.

3 ☐ The park has too many garbage.

4 ☐ Road maintenance costs a few money.

5 ☐ Hardly any aspects of the city are good for children.

6 ☐ There wasn't a few to do in the area.

4 Correct the incorrect sentences in Exercise 3.

5 Use the table and the words in parentheses to complete sentences about changes to a city.

2012	2015
5,000 unemployed people	5,050 unemployed people
Number of buses 3	Number of buses 12
Children's playgrounds 1	Children's playgrounds 4
Air pollution level 5/5	Air pollution level 2/5
Recycling facility 0	Recycling facilities 8

1 In 2015 _____. (a few)

2 In 2012 _____. (many)

3 In 2012 _____. (hardly any)

4 In 2012 _____. (too much)

5 In 2012 _____. (no)

Writing skill

Describing locations and changes

To describe locations on a map or diagram we can use a range of prepositions such as:

next to, between, in front of, across from.

You can also describe the location of features.

In the southeast the fields and trees were replaced by a golf course.

We can use a range of verbs to describe the change.

The warehouse was converted into a spa hotel.

1 Using the icons, complete the sentences with the words in the box.

by   in between   in the northeast   to the south of

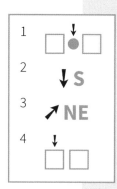

1 The former factory, _____ the warehouse and fields, has been changed into a gym and swimming pool.

2 _____ the river, the whole area has been changed.

3 _____, the fields and trees have been replaced with a new golf course.

4 The former windmill _____ the warehouse is now a restaurant.

2 Match the verbs with their definitions.

1 **adapt**   a to change to another use
2 **construct**   b to make big changes
3 **expand**   c to make longer
4 **extend**   d to build
5 **remove**   e to make bigger
6 **transform**   f to take away

3 Complete the sentences with words from Exercise 2 in the simple past.

1 They _____ the road to reach the new hotel.

2 The park area was _____ to twice its previous size so that the children had more space to play.

3 The local community _____ a children's play area in the south.

4 The old gas station was _____ into a new restaurant to provide social facilities for people.

5 The area was _____ from a former industrial area into a beautiful community space.

6 The trees were _____ and a new swimming pool built in their place.

4 Why do you think the changes were made to the town in Exercise 3? How do you think they have helped improve the town?

Writing task

You are going to describe the changes and improvements to an area of farmland as shown on two plans.

Brainstorm

Look at the two maps. Make notes about the ways the area changed.

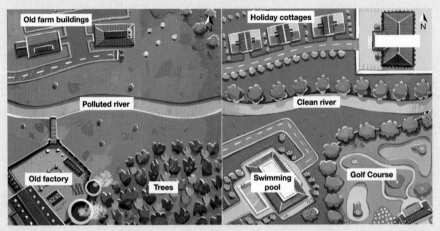

2012   2016

Plan

Answer the following questions as you plan your description.

1   What buildings changed use?
2   What things were added to the area on the map?
3   What things improved?

Write

Using your answers to the questions above, write a description of the changes shown on the two maps. Use words to describe locations and changes. Pay attention to your use of prepositions and determiners of quantity. Your text should be about 150 words long.

Share

Exchange paragraphs with a partner. Look at the checklist on page 189 and provide feedback to your partner.

Rewrite and edit

Read your partner's comments. What could you change to make your writing better? Revise your text, then check it for errors. Think about:
• prepositions and determiners
• words to describe changes and results.

Write the final draft.

Review

Wordlist

MACMILLAN DICTIONARY

Vocabulary preview

ability (n) ***	demolish (v) *	go wrong (phrase)	run-down (adj)
attempt (n) ***	employment (n) ***	green space (n)	succeed (v) ***
believe in (phr v)	failure (n) ***	income (n) ***	transform (v) **
deal with (phr v)	former (adj) ***	opportunity (n) ***	wildlife (n) **

Vocabulary development

react (v) **	rebuild (v) **	redo (v)	replace (v) ***
rearrange (v)	recycle (v) *	renew (v) **	reuse (v)

Academic words

alter (v) **	community (n) ***	maintenance (n) **	reject (v) ***
aspect (n) ***	feature (n) ***	motivation (n) **	transfer (v) ***

Academic words review

Complete the sentences with the words in the box.

alter	constant	maintenance	rejected	transfer

1 Customer: This dress is lovely, but it is a bit too long for me.
   Sales assistant: Don't worry. We can _____ it for you.
2 My boss wants to _____ me to our other office in the south of the country. I'd rather stay here.
3 The proposal for a new highway across the state was _____ because it was too expensive.
4 Regular _____ is vital if you want to keep your car running smoothly.
5 Very small children need _____ care.

Unit review

Reading 1	☐	I can identify and use pronoun reference to navigate a text.
Reading 2	☐	I can identify reasons in a text.
Study skill	☐	I can identify my vision of success as a student and think about ways to achieve it.
Vocabulary	☐	I can use words with *re-* prefixes to describe change.
Grammar	☐	I can use determiners of quantity to describe change.
Writing	☐	I can describe locations and changes based on a plan.

Discussion point

Discuss with a partner.

1 How do you feel mentally and physically when you are under pressure?

2 Do you think pressure is ever positive?

3 Do you think people learn to react like this to pressure or is it a natural human reaction to danger?

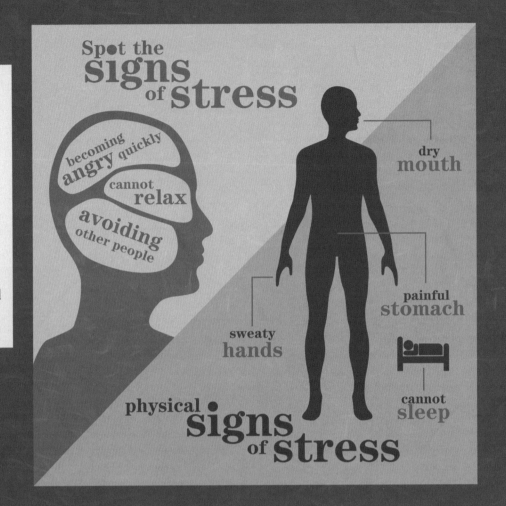

Spot the signs of stress

becoming angry quickly

cannot relax

avoiding other people

dry mouth

painful stomach

sweaty hands

cannot sleep

physical signs of stress

VIDEO

STRESS RELIEF THERAPY

Before you watch

Answer the questions with a partner.

1 How often do you feel under pressure?

2 What things make you feel stressed?

3 What do you do to try to make yourself feel less stressed?

UNIT AIMS

READING 1 Identifying cause and effect
READING 2 Identifying tone
STUDY SKILL Dealing with stress: know your triggers

VOCABULARY Hedging and boosting
GRAMMAR Present conditionals
WRITING Writing about cause and effect

Tennis player Jurgen Melzer under pressure.

While you watch

Read the sentences and then watch the video.
Choose the correct option to complete the sentences.

1 It costs **$2.20 / $11** to smash a plate.

2 Masaki thinks it **is / isn't** a good idea.

3 Smashing plates is supposed to make you feel **happier / less stressed**.

4 A lot of customers are stressed **drivers / businessmen**.

After you watch

Answer the questions with a partner.

1 Do you think this method would make you feel less stressed?

   No, because …   Yes, because …

2 What unusual things do you know that other people do to reduce their stress?

   I know someone who …

3 Why do you think so many people find work stressful?

   They find it stressful because …

Pressure on parents

A Vocabulary preview

1 Complete the questions with the words in the box.

> achievement ambition compare insist
> lifestyle pressure result work-life balance

1 What do you think is more important—_____ or talent?

2 When you feel stressed and have a lot of _____ from work or studying, how do you react?

3 When you last faced a difficult situation, what was the _____ at the end?

4 What was your biggest _____ last year?

5 Do you think you have a good _____ or do you feel you study / work too hard?

6 When you _____ work and studying which one do you think is more stressful?

7 Would you describe your _____ as healthy and calm, or pressured and unhealthy?

8 Do you _____ that other people work long hours when you do a project together?

2 Discuss the questions in Exercise 1 with a partner.

B Before you read

Preparing to read

1 **Think about different members of your family. Write down one or two different pressures each one is under.**

2 **Compare your ideas with a partner. Why do you think each person faces different pressures?**

C Global reading

Summarizing main ideas

Skim *Pressure on parents*. Choose the best summary.

1 The biggest pressure on parents is the work-life balance issue. It is difficult for both parents to work. So either one parent stops working or they pay for expensive childcare. They also have to pay for vacations, clubs, birthdays, and fashionable clothes.

2 Managing the work-life balance is particularly stressful for parents. It also places financial pressure on families. However, perhaps the biggest pressure comes from comparing ourselves to other people. The need to keep up with others and look perfect starts from the birth of a child and continues throughout parenthood.

Pressure on parents

1 It seems modern lives are the reason parents are facing a range of pressures. Reducing their children's time on technology, showing their perfect family life on social media, and going on impressive vacations are all quite new pressures. However, most of these modern-day pressures still go back to two main causes—balancing family life and work, and comparing ourselves to others.

2 Work-life balance is a pressure for most people, but add in everything a family needs as well and this pressure is higher. People can feel guilty or stressed because they might not be doing well at work. This can also lead to pressure on relationships at home. This is especially true for people who have difficulty organizing, planning, and deciding on the most important things to do. If people have poor time-management skills it can lead to them worrying about how well they parent and how well they do their job. They can feel that they do not have time to do either to the best of their ability.

3 It can also be difficult to achieve a good work-life balance due to the financial pressures of modern life. In many countries, it is difficult to pay for a good lifestyle if only one parent works. If both parents work, there is the extra cost of childcare. If only one parent works, the family loses the salary of one individual. Additionally, many parents feel the pressure to pay for and send their children to a good school. This can cause more financial stress for parents.

4 In part, the ambition to earn more money for the family is connected to the other main pressure modern families are under—comparing ourselves to other people. Previously, comparing ourselves would have been limited to those in our neighborhood. As a result of technology and the ability to move further for work, we now compare ourselves to a much wider range of people. Nearly every time we compare ourselves it results in expensive purchases, from wanting to have the same (or even more) impressive vacations to following the latest fashion trends to fit in with others. All are ways of comparing ourselves to others and all result in pressure to earn more money to pay for them.

5 Many ways we compare are financial, but there is no doubt that many feel the pressure from the birth of their first child. Almost as soon as the child is born, the pressure to be the perfect parents often results in worry. Whether it is walking, feeding, or sleeping, there are things people think a baby should be doing by a certain age. Many feel that if their child does not match the "normal" level, then it will look bad for them. The pressure to be perfect is so strong that it leads to many parents lying about how much their baby sleeps at night. Some parents even pay for sleep specialists to help get their baby to sleep. Sleep is usually the one free activity in life.

6 Most of these pressures can possibly be avoided if people make one small change in their view of life—stop comparing yourself to others. Then there would be less pressure to be "perfect" and more opportunities to simply enjoy your time together.

GLOSSARY

childcare (n) the job of looking after children, especially while their parents are working

Identifying cause and effect

D Close reading

> Causes (that make something happen) and effects (the results of what happened) can often be identified by looking for signal words. For example: *because, due to, reason, result, leads to.*
>
> We also use conditional sentences (*if* sentences) to show cause and effect relationships, e.g.
>
> *If you don't get enough sleep [cause], you feel tired [effect].*

1   Look at these sentences from *Pressure on parents*. Underline the cause and circle the effect.

    1   It seems modern lives are the reason parents are facing a range of pressures.

    2   It can also be difficult to achieve a good work-life balance due to the financial pressures of modern life.

    3   In many countries, it is difficult to pay for a good lifestyle if only one parent works.

    4   All are ways of comparing ourselves to others and all result in pressure to earn more money to pay for them.

    5   The pressure to be perfect is so strong that it leads to many parents lying about how much their baby sleeps at night.

2   Read the text again. Match the causes and effects in these sentences.

    1   Not doing your job well ____

    2   Poor time management skills ____

    3   Because of childcare costs or the loss of a salary ____

    4   Technology means ____

    5   Most comparisons happen because ____

    a   families can feel under financial pressure.

    b   can lead to poor relationships at home.

    c   of expensive purchases, like vacations and fashionable clothes.

    d   can result in people worrying about their performance at work.

    e   we compare ourselves to a wide group of people.

E Critical thinking

In your country, what can be done to reduce pressure on parents?

Study skills | Dealing with stress: know your triggers

1 Look at these examples of feeling under pressure. Circle the ones that are true for you.

> exam deadlines   someone disliking a social media post
> tuition fees   work-life balance

2 Add any other things that cause you stress to the list.

3 Tell a partner how you feel about it.

4 Read *Dealing with stress: know your triggers*. Check (✓) the "triggers" in the box that affect you in the situations in Exercise 1. Compare them with a partner.

5 Write down three tips for dealing with deadline or exam stress. Work in groups and choose the best five tips to share with the class.

Rich and famous

A Vocabulary preview

1 Match the words in bold with the correct definitions.

1	**celebrity** (n)	a	the time of your life when you are very young
2	**childhood** (n)	b	to continue happening or existing for a period of time
3	**last** (v)	c	the feeling of pleasure that you get when you achieve or obtain something that you want
4	**limited** (adj)		
5	**put in** (phr v)	d	not very great in amount
6	**satisfaction** (n)	e	a famous person, especially in entertainment or sports
7	**status** (n)	f	someone's position in a profession or society, especially compared with other people
8	**youth** (n)		
		g	the time of your life when you are young
		h	to give time or effort to something

2 Complete the sentences with words from Exercise 1.

1 Too many children want to become a _____. They should focus on getting a real job.

2 College does not _____ long enough. Five or six years would be better.

3 There are _____ jobs available so you must choose your college degree carefully.

4 Molly must _____ the hours if she wants to pass her driving test.

5 People get _____ from achieving even simple things.

6 Too many people want to grow up quickly, but it's important to enjoy your _____.

7 In my _____, probably until my mid-twenties, I was a lot more relaxed and less stressed.

8 People often compare their _____ and what they have achieved with others.

3 What pressures and stresses do you think are different for young people?

B Before you read

Preparing to read

1 Discuss these questions with a partner.

1 What jobs do most young children in your country want to have?

2 Do you think the following can be considered jobs?

> actor athlete pop star

2 Why are the jobs above difficult to get? What problems might this cause?

Rich and famous

1 **If you could have any job in the world, what would it be? This is a common question often asked during childhood in many cultures. Children have been asked this question for generations, but their answers are changing. Recent studies have highlighted a dramatic and rather worrying shift in children's ambitions.**

2 Twenty-five years ago, the most common ambition of American children was to be a teacher, followed by working in banking and finance, and then medicine. Today's younger generation often say they want to be a sports star, a pop star, or an actor. In the U.K., talent shows are also affecting children's career choices, with many wanting to be professional dancers, like those they see on television and read about in the media. While many argue that there is nothing wrong with having big ambitions, this worrying trend could lead to people feeling unhappy as more and more are unable to reach their goals.

3 Some surveys have found that children want these jobs largely because of the high levels of money connected with them. That does not mean they are willing to work for the increased wealth. To achieve these lifestyles often requires people to put in many hours of work, but it seems many are not willing to put in the work. A good work-life balance is often considered more important. People want a lot of free time to enjoy their life and therefore do not want a job to take over, even if the money is great. Clearly, there is an increasing gap between wanting wealth and money and the willingness to work for it.

4 However, according to experts, big ambitions put pressures on the individual. Julian Rotter, an American psychologist, suggested a theory in which people decide how likely they are to achieve a goal before they make the effort to achieve it. If people link happiness to money and status, they are more likely to work hard to achieve them. However, the satisfaction does not last long because once a person meets their goal, they no longer have a sense of satisfaction. This then creates a pressure for the person to keep pushing to achieve more goals, which places that person under greater stress.

5 Clearly, even if young people are willing to put in the work to train, the chances of success are small. Many professional soccer clubs' youth programs work with children as young as eight. Every year, the unwanted players are asked to leave the club. At the age of 12, those who are still there sign two-year contracts with no confirmed future career. Only a very small percentage of people will ever actually become professional soccer players. Access to other celebrity professions doesn't always end so quickly but is still very difficult. Being an actor does not mean playing for just one team so you can always keep trying. However, the chances of success are again very small and many actors will earn an extremely low salary rather than the imagined Hollywood money. In fact, most will have salaries only slightly better than window cleaners, waiters, and hairdressers.

6 Unfortunately, fame and fortune are not always good for everyone. Many careers of famous people are short-lived. For example, many athletes' physical peak only lasts a few years, and singers can have a very limited career. The job that was once the only focus of their lives becomes something they are no longer involved with. As a result, they can feel a complete lack of control and as if they are not good enough. It can also be difficult for them to go back to a normal everyday life because they have been living a very different one for so long.

7 So despite the apparent problems of being rich and famous, there is greater ambition than ever among young people to get to that position. In many ways, this has been brought about by cultural changes. Globally, more and more TV shows feature talent competitions where winners can achieve wealth and fame in just a few weeks or months. This quick route to fame and fortune creates a celebrity culture. People are not very realistic and believe that a celebrity lifestyle is easy to get and leads to great satisfaction. It is perhaps not surprising that this is especially attractive in societies where youth unemployment is between 25% and 50%.

8 It is no longer enough to have simple ambitions. People are not satisfied just to make a living—they want to be rich. In the past, people had more modest, sensible aims such as earning good wages, not being unemployed, and enjoying their work. Job satisfaction was important. Parents and teachers, rather than TV, had a greater impact on children's ambitions. Unfortunately, not everyone realizes that it takes talent, skill, and hard work to be good at a sport or at singing. As a result, many people won't achieve their childhood dreams, and this can have a negative effect on their happiness.

GLOSSARY

celebrity culture (n) a consumer interest in celebrity lifestyles

salary (n) the fixed amount of money you receive from your employer, normally every month

C Global reading

> Authors do not always state their opinion clearly but we can infer how they feel from the language they use. Noticing positive or negative phrases as well as adjectives and adverbs, e.g. *dramatic, worrying, shocking, exciting* can tell you if the text has a positive or negative tone and help you infer the author's opinion.
>
> Understanding an author's opinion is important if you use a text for research because it will give you an idea whether the writer is for or against a certain position.

1 Read *Rich and famous* quickly and decide whether the author has a positive or negative opinion about the following topics.

   1 The change in the things children want (paragraph 2)
   2 How children view hard work today (paragraph 3)
   3 The belief that it is easy to become a celebrity (paragraph 5)
   4 People's job choices in the past (paragraph 8)

2 Read the text again and underline adjectives, adverbs, and phrases that show the author's opinion.

D Close reading

Read *Rich and famous* again. Write *T* (True), *F* (False), or *NG* (Not Given) for each sentence.

1 Young people's ambitions have changed. ___
2 Children are happy to work hard for fame and wealth. ___
3 Once we achieve a goal we then set new ones. ___
4 Young soccer players are not successful because they don't train hard. ___
5 Most actors earn high salaries. ___
6 People find it easy to go back to a normal life after a successful career in sports or entertainment. ___
7 Fame and fortune make people feel happy. ___
8 Parents do not have a large impact on their children's ambitions anymore. ___

E Critical thinking

Discuss these questions in a group.

1 Is it healthy for children to desire celebrity jobs? Why / why not?
2 To what extent do parents and teachers influence children's ambitions?

Vocabulary development

Hedging and boosting

We can use a range of expressions to make an opinion stronger or weaker in an essay.

Hedging phrases and words make our opinion more cautious and show we are not sure, e.g.

*Life today is **possibly** more stressful than 50 years ago.*

Boosting phrases and words make our opinion stronger, e.g.

***Certainly**, comparing ourselves to others adds stress to our life.*

1 Complete the table with the words and phrases in the box.

> clearly   definitely   is believed   is thought
> may   might   no doubt that   surely

Hedging	Boosting
possibly	*certainly*

2 Choose the best way to complete the sentences. Do you agree or disagree with each one?

1 **Clearly / No doubt that**, being a doctor is one of the most stressful jobs.

2 It **is believed / might** young people want to be rich and famous.

3 Family life **might / is thought** to be more stressful than work.

4 There is **may / no doubt that** coursework shows a student's ability better than an exam.

5 Hard work **might / surely** be more important than luck in being successful.

6 **May / Surely** pressure is one of the biggest health concerns in the modern world.

7 There **may / clearly** be less stress in the modern world than in the past.

8 There is **believed / definitely** a lot of pressure on young people to go to college.

3 Add a hedging or boosting phrase to the sentences below to match your opinion.

1 Modern life is more pressured than life 50 years ago.

2 People are more interested in money than anything else.

3 Exams are too stressful and should not happen.

4 Compare your sentences with a partner. Discuss the reasons for your opinion.

Academic words

1 Match the words in bold with the correct definitions.

1 **apparent** (adj)
2 **confirmed** (adj)
3 **dramatic** (adj)
4 **focus** (n)
5 **highlight** (v)
6 **media** (n)
7 **shift** (n)
8 **theory** (n)

a the thing that people are concentrating on or paying particular attention to

b radio, television, newspapers, the Internet, and magazines, considered as a group: can be followed by a singular or plural verb

c proven and therefore known to be true or accurate

d a change in an idea, attitude, or plan

e easy to see and understand

f sudden and surprising or easy to notice

g one or more ideas that explain how or why something happens

h to describe something in a way that makes people notice and think about it

2 Complete the sentences with words from Exercise 1.

1 One _____ suggests that people do not feel happy because they compare themselves to others.

2 The newspaper published a _____ story that they knew was true.

3 There has been a _____ rise in unemployment since 2007. It has risen by over 40%.

4 The _____ use celebrities to sell newspapers.

5 The _____ of the study was on how stress affects the happiness of young children.

6 The news story _____ how big the influence of celebrity image is on young people.

7 Marcus has headaches, is pale, and cannot focus. It should be _____ he is under a lot of pressure.

8 There has been a _____ in attitudes towards being a celebrity in recent years. Many young people now see it as a possible job.

3 Tell your partner about one theory you know from your studies. What was the focus? What did it highlight? Does it explain any dramatic shifts from what was known before?

Writing model

You are going to learn about present conditionals and how to write cause and effect paragraphs in order to write about the causes and effects of pressure on children.

A Model

Read the model answer. Which essay question do you think the paragraphs relate to?

1 What are the effects of pressure from social media and modern technology on young people?

2 What are the advantages and disadvantages of social media?

3 To what extent should social media be restricted for young people?

> One of the main causes of pressure on children today is the increased use of social media. Nowadays children spend many hours interacting with social media platforms. It is thought this has led to pressures to maintain a particular image. If children share an image or video online, the number of likes or comments can have a dramatic effect on how they feel about themselves. They also feel under pressure to maintain a particular image to show how exciting their lifestyle is. As a result, there is a constant focus on their social lives and they feel judged about their vacations and the things they like and do.
>
> In addition to pressures from social media, children are feeling increasing pressure from living in an environment where they are always in contact with people. Previously, if a child had a difficult time with friends, they could leave this behind at school. The shift to smartphones has meant that this has become increasingly difficult. A number of surveys have highlighted how not being able to switch off and walk away has increased stress levels for children. If technological access were limited, it would significantly reduce stress levels for young people.

B Analyze

1 **Read the model again and answer the questions.**

   1 What are the two main causes of pressure on children described in the paragraphs?

   2 What are the two main effects described in the paragraphs?

2 **Discuss these questions with a partner.**

   1 What other pressures are children under?

   2 Which factors do you think cause the most pressure?

   3 What are the biggest effects of pressure on children?

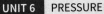

Grammar

Present conditionals

We use a different conditional depending on whether we are talking about a real or imaginary situation. We use the **present real conditional** to talk about events that are *likely* to happen, and the **present unreal conditional** to talk about events that are *unlikely* to happen.

Form	Examples
Present real conditional *If* clause result clause simple present + *will* / another modal verb	*If you are under pressure, you will not be able to work well.* *If you use social media regularly, you may worry about other people's opinions more.* *What will happen if children continue to face this pressure?*
Present unreal conditional *If* clause result clause simple past + *would* / *might* / *could*	*If we didn't put so much academic pressure on children, they wouldn't feel as stressed.* *If children were encouraged to exercise more, they would feel less worried.* *How might children feel if other people's opinions were not so important?*

1 Read the situations. Is the situation *R* (Real) or *U* (Unreal)?

1 If I get good grades, I will go to college. ___

2 If I didn't have a good car, I wouldn't be so popular. ___

3 If I posted this online, people wouldn't like it. ___

4 If I don't work hard, I won't pass the test. ___

5 If we win the game, everyone will be happy. ___

6 If I had more money, I would buy better clothes. ___

2 Complete the conditional sentences with the correct form of the verbs in parentheses. Use the word in italics to help you choose the conditional form.

1 If I _____ (work) hard, I _____ (feel) more stressed. *real*

2 If I _____ (graduate) with a good degree, I _____ (have) a better chance of a good job. *real*

3 I _____ (be) less stressed if I _____ (have) different friends. *unreal*

4 If someone _____ (have) more exams, they _____ (be) more stressed. *real*

5 If I _____ (not go) on social media, I _____ (feel) under less pressure. *unreal*

3 Correct the mistakes in these present unreal conditional sentences.

1 If I could have any job in the world, I would to be a doctor.

2 If I had my own business, it will be a store.

3 I would felt less stressed if I had more free time.

4 If I could bought anything in the world, I would buy a sports car.

5 I would be happier if I would be healthier.

6 If I was under pressure, I take a vacation.

4 Rewrite the sentences in Exercise 3 so that they are true for you.

5 Work with a partner and ask them questions to find out what they would do in each of the situations in Exercises 3 and 4.

Writing skill

> When writing paragraphs on causes and effects, it is a good idea to focus on one cause and its effects in one paragraph and then describe a different cause and its effects in the second paragraph.
>
> We use a range of language to link causes and effects:
>
> **Causes:** *one cause is, another cause, one reason is, due to, owing to, as a result of*
>
> **Effects:** *this means that, therefore, consequently, result in*

1 Reorder the sentences to form two paragraphs.

A It is believed that some parents compare their children to others at school because they want their child to get the best scores in tests. ___

B Another reason for pressure on children is increased use of social media. ___

C One cause of pressure on children comes from parents wanting children to be successful in everything they do. ___

D Children constantly see perfect versions of people's lives. ___

E Consequently, the children will feel like they have failed if they do not get the highest scores in the class. ___

F As a result, children put more pressure on themselves to look perfect in their own photos. ___

2 Choose the correct words or phrases to complete the cause and effect sentences.

1 **Due to / Result in** increased pressure, many students do not sleep well.

2 **Owing to / One cause of** stress is wanting to be popular among other people.

3 **As a result of / Resulting in** technology, people compare themselves to others more often.

4 We see the lives of the rich and famous and **therefore / this means that** want a similar life for ourselves.

5 **Result in / Consequently**, parents worry and put even more pressure on young people to do well.

3 Look at these causes of stress. Discuss the effects of each with a partner.

1 Smartphone use

2 Long journeys to work

3 Two parents working

Writing task

Use present conditionals to write two cause and effect paragraphs in answer to the question:

"Discuss the causes and effects of pressure on children today".

Brainstorm

Complete the brainstorm below.

Causes	Effects

Plan

1 Which causes and effects will you focus on?

2 How are the causes and effects connected?

3 Which causes and effects will you describe in each paragraph?

Write

Using your answers to the questions above, write two paragraphs on the essay question: *"Discuss the causes and effects of pressure on children today".* Remember to organize your causes and effects appropriately. Pay attention to your use of real and unreal conditionals to talk about cause and effect. Your text should be 150 to 200 words long.

Share

Exchange paragraphs with a partner. Look at the checklist on page 189 and provide feedback to your partner.

Rewrite and edit

Read your partner's comments. What could you change to make your writing better? Revise your text, then check it for errors. Think about:

- the organization of your ideas
- your use of real and unreal conditionals.

Write the final draft.

Review

Wordlist

MACMILLAN DICTIONARY

Vocabulary preview

achievement (n) ***	compare (v) ***	limited (adj) ***	satisfaction (n) **
ambition (n) **	insist (v) ***	pressure (n) ***	status (n) ***
celebrity (n) *	last (v) ***	put in (phrase v)	work-life balance (n)
childhood (n) **	lifestyle (n) **	result (n) ***	youth (n) ***

Vocabulary development

clearly (adv) ***	is believed (phrase)	may (mod v) ***	no doubt that (phrase)
definitely (adv) **	is thought (phrase)	might (mod v)	surely (adv) ***

Academic words

apparent (adj) ***	dramatic (adj) ***	highlight (v) **	shift (n) **
confirmed (adj)	focus (n) ***	media (n) ***	theory (n) ***

Academic words review

Complete the sentences with the words in the box.

apparent   highlighted   investment   media   seek

1 The newspaper article _____ the challenges falling oil prices presented to the economy.

2 It was _____ from the cracks in the walls that the building was not safe and was a danger to the public.

3 Do you think stocks and share are a good _____ or do you think they are too risky?

4 Adam didn't know what to do, so he decided to _____ advice from a lawyer.

5 Do you use social _____, such as Facebook and Twitter?

Unit review

Reading 1		I can identify cause and effect in a text.
Reading 2		I can infer the tone of a text to understand the writer's opinion.
Study skill		I can recognize my triggers to help me deal with stress.
Vocabulary		I can use hedging and boosting vocabulary to make an opinion stronger or weaker.
Grammar		I can use present conditionals to describe real and unreal situations.
Writing		I can write paragraphs describing causes and effects.

WHAT ARE YOU *AFRAID OF?*

Discussion point

Discuss with a partner.

1 Have you met anyone who has any of the fears in the infographic?

2 Why do you think people have these fears?

3 Why do you think so many people are scared of different animals?

FIVE COMMON FEARS

1 **aerophobia:** *fear of flying*
Fear of flying is often connected to other fears, such as fear of small spaces.

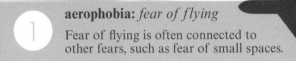

2 **mysophobia:** *fear of germs*
People with this fear often wash a lot and think carefully about what they eat.

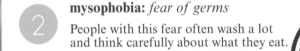

3 **astraphobia:** *fear of thunder and lightning*
It is often children who have astraphobia, but some adults have it too.

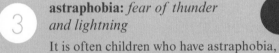

4 **acrophobia:** *fear of heights*
Most people are cautious in high places but acrophobia can cause serious panic.

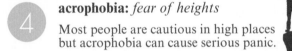

5 **arachnophobia:** *fear of spiders*
Even though most spiders are not dangerous this is one of the most common fears.

VIDEO

ARACHNOPHOBIA

Before you watch

Work with a partner. Rank the ideas for dealing with a fear from the best to worst.

a Face the fear, e.g. hold a spider, stand on a tall building. ___

b Breathe calmly and walk around slowly. ___

c Imagine a happy place. ___

High-wire artist Kane Peterson in Melbourne, Australia.

While you watch

Read the sentences and then watch the video.
Choose the correct option to complete the sentences.

1   Most spiders **are / aren't** dangerous.

2   Spiders **are / aren't** important for growing food.

3   The exhibition wants people to think spiders are
likely to **help / harm** us.

After you watch

Answer the questions with a partner.

1   Do you think spiders should be protected because
of their importance? Why?

2   Why do you think so many people are scared
of spiders?

They find them scary because …

3   Do you think the exhibition will help people who
have a fear of spiders?

I do / don't think it will help because …

Fears, learning, coping

A Vocabulary preview

1 Complete the sentences with the words and phrases in the box.

| breathing exercises | cope | extreme | face | get over | harm | panic | phobia |

1 The best way to _____ a fear is to put yourself in the situation that makes you afraid.

2 It's important to control your feelings when you have to _____ a fear.

3 _____ can help to keep you calm. They relax you and allow you to focus.

4 When people see someone _____ they react in a worried and stressed way as well.

5 People who can't _____ with and manage their fears need to seek help.

6 Fear is normal, but a _____ is more serious and can change your life.

7 A lot of people are scared of things that are safe and cannot _____ us.

8 My fear of flying is very _____. I avoid traveling because it is so bad.

2 Check (✓) the sentences you agree with. Discuss your choices with a partner.

B Before you read

Preparing to read

Look at these situations. What fear might each one cause?

1 Being bitten by an animal as a child

2 Being embarrassed in front of a lot of people

3 Getting lost in a large place such as a mall

This might make you afraid of …

C Global reading

Using topic sentences

1 Underline the topic sentence in each paragraph of *Fears, learning, coping*.

2 Use the topic sentences to identify the main idea of each paragraph.

Fears, learning, coping

1. Many people have a fear of things like snakes, spiders, heights, water, and small spaces. If many people have the same fears, how do we all develop them?

2. If you think about the time when we did not live in houses, but in nature, we faced many more dangers from animals. Because of this, we developed a response to situations to protect ourselves from things that might injure or harm us, such as a bite from a poisonous snake or encountering a dangerous dog. Of course, not all fears are something we have had from birth. For example, if you see someone in trouble in water or almost drown, you may react by developing a fear of water. Or, if a parent has a fear of heights, it is quite common for their children to also develop a fear of heights. The cause of this is not genetic. We are not born with this fear because of our parents. It is because children have learned behavior and attitudes from their parents.

3. One important thing to consider is the difference between what we call a fear and what we consider a phobia. While almost everyone has a fear of something, a fear is only classified as a phobia by psychologists if it is so serious it causes you problems in your daily life. The Anxiety Disorders Association of America has claimed that 19 million Americans (around 6% of the population) have certain phobias, such as crossing bridges or traveling through tunnels. Another 15 million (around 5%) have a social phobia such as public speaking. Unfortunately, those who have one phobia are likely to have others too.

4. Because many fears are learned during our lives, we just have to learn different ways of coping and adjust our attitudes to the things we are afraid of. If people confront their fear in small ways, they can learn to control how they react to the situation and not panic. It might not stop the fear completely, but it will probably help people to cope better and to focus on other issues. Many people manage to reduce fears they have experienced for a long time by using a variety of practices. Some people do something else to stop them thinking about the fear, others use breathing exercises and imagine themselves in a happy place.

5. People have different ways of coping. Some people cope by thinking about the proof. If you're scared of being in a broken elevator and running out of air, think whether this has ever happened to anyone. Many people have a fear of sharks, but they are thought to kill just five people a year. It is believed you are more likely to be killed by a snack vending machine falling on top of you.

6. One of the most extreme ways of dealing with a fear is to face your fears directly. As a child, Alain Robert was afraid of heights, but he dealt with the fear when he couldn't get into his parents' seventh-floor apartment and climbed the building to get in. Since then, he has climbed some of the world's tallest landmarks including Chicago's Sears Tower and the Eiffel Tower in Paris. Facing your fears might make you achieve things you never thought were possible.

GLOSSARY

drown (v) to die by sinking under water

vending machine (n) a machine you can buy things from like candy or drinks

Deducing meaning
from context

D Close reading

You do not need to know every word in a paragraph to understand the general meaning. You can also use the words you do know, sentences before and after the word, and the main ideas of the paragraph to help you work out the meaning of new words.

1 Find the following words in *Fears, learning, coping*. Use the context of the paragraphs to help you choose the correct definition for each word.

1 **genetic** (paragraph 2) ___　　　4 **practices** (paragraph 4) ___

2 **classified** (paragraph 3) ___　　5 **proof** (paragraph 5) ___

3 **confront** (paragraph 4) ___　　　6 **landmarks** (paragraph 6) ___

a to face or deal with a problem

b an activity or way of doing something

c things we are born with because of our parents

d a famous building or sight

e information or evidence that shows that something is definitely true or exists

f to put people or things into groups

2 Answer the questions using no more than three words from the text.

1 What fear might you develop if you see someone almost drown?

   _____

2 What do children learn about fears from their parents? _____

3 What kind of phobia do 15 million Americans have? _____

4 What won't happen if you control your fear? _____

5 What kills more people than sharks every year? _____

E Critical thinking

Answer the questions in groups.

1 What behaviors and attitudes do you think children learn about fear?

2 Do you think people can change our attitudes to fears if we want to? Why / why not?

   As far as I'm concerned, phobias can be learned because …

   I definitely feel that phobias can be unlearned because …

Study skills	Giving and receiving feedback and criticism

It can be hard to hear any criticism, whether positive, in the form of compliments, or as areas for improvement. However, we can learn a great deal if we are prepared to listen to feedback.

- Be open to hearing what people say, even if you find it difficult to sit through.
- Assume that the person giving feedback wants to help you and is on your side, even if it doesn't feel like it.
- Listen carefully. Take time to think about what has been said. Look for the truth in it.
- Hear the main message, rather than questioning whether the speaker has understood everything about your intentions or the issue.

© Stella Cottrell (2013)

1 Think about when you get feedback on written work from your teachers. Which comment best matches how you feel?

I feel scared. How bad is this going to be?

I feel stressed. This is going to affect my future.

I feel angry. I did a lot of work and don't want anything but a good mark.

I feel positive. I want to learn and get better.

2 Why do you think people often feel worried about receiving feedback?

3 Read *Giving and receiving feedback and criticism*. Which of the tips do you follow? Compare your ideas with a partner.

4 Tell your partner about the last time you received feedback. Discuss these questions:

1 How did you feel?
2 Do you think you could or should respond differently in the future?
3 How can the person giving feedback make it easier?

Fight or flight

A Vocabulary preview

1 Match the words in bold with the correct definitions.

1	**calm** (adj)	a	the power and enthusiasm for wanting to do something
2	**defense** (n)	b	frightened or worried
3	**energy** (n)	c	to keep someone or something safe from harm, injury, damage, or loss
4	**escape** (v)		
5	**hormone** (n)	d	to get away from something especially danger
6	**protect** (v)	e	the way you feel or behave because of something that happens
7	**reaction** (n)		
8	**scared** (adj)	f	action you take to save yourself or someone else from danger
		g	not affected by strong emotions
		h	a chemical made in plants, people, and animals that controls how we feel and act

2 Complete the sentences with words from Exercise 1 in the correct form.

1 The fear gave them the _____ to move quickly.

2 It's natural to try to _____ and run away from danger.

3 When some animals are _____ they stop moving until the danger has passed.

4 The biologist is studying the _____ and chemicals that make us feel worried.

5 Animals try to _____ their young in a dangerous situation.

6 He has a very serious _____ to flying that makes him feel sick. It's a bad phobia.

7 She rushed to her friend's _____ when she was in danger.

8 It is important to remain _____ when you speak in front of a lot of people, but it is difficult.

3 Describe how you feel and your reactions in each of these situations.

1 Facing a dangerous animal

2 Giving a presentation

3 Being trapped in an elevator

B Before you read

Preparing to read

Discuss these questions with a partner.

1 What fears do your friends and family have?

2 What reactions do they have to their fears?

FIGHT OR FLIGHT

GLOSSARY

electric shock (n) a sudden flow of electricity that causes pain

1 **Most people connect fear with negative feelings, but it can actually be very positive as well. Fear is natural and something we are born with. We have always needed it to keep us safe from danger. If we face a dangerous situation, we can find abilities that we often do not know we have.**

2 In the past, humans faced danger every day so they learned to respond to it straight away to stay alive. This natural reaction can also be seen in many animals. Take cuttlefish, an animal in the same family as a squid and octopus. These creatures have an amazing ability to change color and shape. They use this to both fight and escape. With the help of their bright colors, they make other fish slower and easier to catch. Their color also helps them to hide in their environment. Another fish, the electric eel, uses its electric shock to catch food and for self-defense, as an action to protect itself from others. Humans might not have such unusual responses but they do still have a fight or flight instinct, which is the body's natural way of keeping us safe by either facing the danger or getting away from it as quickly as possible.

3 Our bodies react in a number of different ways when we are in a dangerous situation. For example, our reactions often become faster, we become stronger and have more energy. Under pressure we become nervous and some simple skills such as putting a key in a door often become worse. However, physical abilities such as running and jumping tend to improve. If an angry dog chases you, you will probably run away from it faster. In a normal situation we often only use 65% of our strength, but studies have shown that this can increase to as much as 85% in more dangerous situations.

4 So how does our body create such a reaction? Fear is a natural reaction in the brain to an external stressful or dangerous situation and is the body's internal way of trying to stay calm. Hormones are released that cause our heart to beat faster and our breathing to become quicker. This response is known as the fight or flight response and it makes it difficult to remain calm. Instead, you might run away or fight the situation that scared you. The fight or flight response is a very quick reaction that happens before you are aware of it. The brain reacts a little more slowly. When the brain processes the situation it can decide, based on experience, if there is no danger. The first increase of energy then stops and you feel calmer again.

5 In biology, the brain causes the body to release over 30 different hormones, such as adrenaline, a chemical that gives you more energy when frightened, excited, or angry, to help keep us safe. These hormones cause a range of reactions. Some senses such as our eyes change to let more light in. Some of our body relaxes to let more air in. Other parts of the body become tense because of the adrenaline and glucose, a sugar produced in the body. More blood is sent to our muscles and organs, for example, the heart and other parts of the body that do specific jobs to keep us alive. We often feel cold and connect fear with being cold because our bodies are keeping us and our organs safe, instead of keeping us warm. It is also why we feel tired when we recover from a shock. Fear is designed to protect us.

6 Although we might not face as many physical dangers today as we did in the past, fear still helps to keep us safe. It stops us from doing stupid things, like walking out into a busy road or not being careful on a high building. It limits the risks that we are willing to take. However, these limits may also take away some opportunities in our lives. One common fear is a fear of failure. Many people are not willing to take risks because they are too scared of failing. This fear can lead to people not taking good chances. The risk of making a mistake is minimized, but it also means people are less likely to try new things and may achieve less. This desire to avoid failure can make people act differently to when they feel more confident.

7 While fear may make people work slowly, and even limit opportunities in life, it can also make us better at certain things. People who experience fear often are usually better at making decisions as they understand the risk more quickly. If people always only see the positives in things, they may not pay attention to negative information they receive. As a result, this can make them poor decision makers.

8 When we combine anxiety and fear with training, the results can be even more positive. If we are well-trained and prepared, we can react to stressful situations in a normal and calm way. Fear and adrenaline from the fight or flight instinct make you quick to respond to things while training means you know what to do. This is why emergency professionals train for a wide range of situations and can remain calm when most of us would panic. Fear can be used to your advantage as long as you plan ahead and do your research.

C Global reading

Skim each paragraph in *Fight or flight* and identify in which paragraph you could find the information to answer these questions.

1 What is the body naturally trying to do when we feel fear?
2 What things can fear stop us doing today?
3 Which animal changes color to keep it safe?
4 What can fear make us better at?
5 What happens to our reactions when we are in danger?
6 How can training help us deal with situations many fear?
7 How do biology and hormones affect our eyes when we are in danger?

D Close reading

1 Read the text and answer the questions in *C Global reading*.

> While it is often possible to use the context of a paragraph to find the meaning of new words, sometimes unusual words are defined in the text. This is often true if the words are very specific and unlikely to be known, for example with scientific vocabulary. There might be full definitions where the meaning of the word is explained, e.g.
>
> *When an animal is scared, it will try to escape, **get away from something**.*
>
> Or the new words can be defined using examples:
>
> *In an emergency it is important to have a calm reaction, **like speaking softly to someone who is hurt**.*

2 Work with a partner. Student A find the definitions for 1–3. Student B find the definitions for 4–6.

1 self-defense
2 fight or flight instinct
3 physical abilities
4 adrenaline
5 glucose
6 organs

3 Try to explain the meaning of the words in Exercise 2 to your partner.

E Critical thinking

1 *Fight or flight* claims that fear can stop us from taking risks. Do you think avoiding risk is a good or bad thing?

2 Do you agree that fear stops people from achieving what they want to? What examples can you think of?

Vocabulary development

Verb and preposition collocations

Many words commonly collocate (are used together) with another word. Collocations are sometimes different in other languages. For accuracy in English, it is important to learn which words go together.

1 Read the sentences and choose the correct preposition to complete each collocation in bold.

1 To get good grades, you need to pay attention and **focus to / on** your work.

2 I'm really worried because the teacher is going to **comment for / on** our work today. I don't like getting feedback.

3 I have a few fears, but I really **suffer from / of** a fear of small spaces.

4 It took me a while to **recover from / out** the shock, but I feel fine now.

5 My normal response to danger is to **run away from / to** the situation.

6 It's natural to try to **protect** others **of / from** danger.

7 I got over my fear of spiders **with the help of / for** friends.

8 One way to stay calm is to **breathe to and from / in and out**.

2 Complete the advice below with collocations from Exercise 1.

1 Try to think about and _____ a happy place or experience. It will keep you calm.

2 If you _____ a phobia, speak to your doctor.

3 If you don't like a situation, you should walk _____ it and go somewhere else.

4 _____ other people it is possible to get over any fear.

5 Try to _____ for five seconds and _____ for five seconds to feel more relaxed.

6 Don't _____ other people's fears in a negative way. It won't help them.

7 It's not always a good idea to try to _____ someone _____ their phobias. Sometimes they need to face their fear.

8 It can take time to _____ feeling scared. Allow plenty of time to calm down.

3 Look at these situations. Discuss with a partner the best advice to help with these.

1 Finding a large spider in the bath

2 Being stuck in a broken elevator

3 Being outside in a storm

Academic words

1 Match the words in bold with the correct definitions.

1 **adjust** (v)
2 **aware** (adj)
3 **encounter** (v)
4 **external** (adj)
5 **injure** (v)
6 **internal** (adj)
7 **minimize** (v)
8 **response** (n)

a to hurt someone or damage their body
b to experience or deal with something, especially a problem
c existing or happening inside a place or a person's body
d a reaction or an answer to an action or question
e to change something slightly
f knowing about a situation or fact
g coming from outside a place or a person's body
h to make something seem much less harmful or important

2 Complete the sentences with words from Exercise 1 in the correct form.

1 Our fears can be _____ through training so they are less strong.
2 When I _____ a spider I am terrified.
3 My _____ to fear is usually to remain calm.
4 We cannot control our _____ environment so we need to control our reactions.
5 We can control our _____ reactions by staying focused and breathing in and out slowly.
6 When I am _____ of danger I usually try to face it.
7 It is silly to be scared of something that cannot harm or _____ you.
8 When you have had a phobia for a long time, it is impossible to _____ your reactions.

3 Check (✓) the sentences you agree with in Exercise 2. Compare and discuss your choices with a partner.

I agree with the idea that … because …
I don't agree with the idea that … because …

Writing model

You are going to learn about the present perfect simple. You are then going to learn to organize your notes into paragraphs and write two paragraphs to answer the question: *"Fear is always bad for us. Describe the pros and cons of fear."*

A Analyze

1   Look at the notes about fear and circle the ideas that are useful for an essay about the pros and cons of fearing failure.

remain calm in an emergency

won't apply for job

scared to take tests

human fear

breathe in and out to stay calm

fear keeps us safe from danger

FEAR OF FAILURE

don't make mistakes

miss opportunities

can start in childhood

think clearly

do excellent work

2   Use your answers to decide on the pros and cons of fearing failure.

B Model

1   Read the model. Underline the pros and circle the cons of fearing failure.

2   Do the pros and cons in the model match your own ideas?

> Fear of failure can negatively affect people in many ways and cause them to miss opportunities in life. People who suffer from this fear often minimize their chances of encountering a situation where they risk failing. Studies have shown that people with a fear of failure are less likely to apply for better jobs and build the careers they want. People could miss other goals like getting into their first choice of college if they are scared to take the tests. Someone with a serious phobia of failing might have avoided activities for most of their lives because their fear has been so extreme. Fear of failure can have serious consequences unless people learn to cope with it.
>
> However, fear of failure can also help people to succeed. Think of someone who has always done well at work and has never made a mistake. That person might have a fear of failure and so they have taken extra care over their tasks. Under pressure you are also able to think more clearly as your mind stops you focusing on things that are not important. So someone who has a fear of failure is less likely to be distracted because of the pressure they put on themselves. Therefore, while fear of failure does have a negative impact it can also help us in many ways.

Grammar

Present perfect simple

We use the present perfect to talk about events that happened at an unspecified point in time, or to connect the past with the present.

In academic writing, the present perfect is also often used to report research findings.

Studies have shown that this can increase to as much as 85% in more dangerous situations.

Form	Examples
have / has + past participle	*We can develop the fear after **we have seen** something that makes us scared.* * **We have developed** a response to situations that might cause us harm.*

For and *since*

We use specific words to describe durations with the present perfect simple. We use *since* to talk about *when* something started and *for* to talk about *how long* something has lasted.

Form	Examples
present perfect + **since** + point in time	*I've been scared of dogs **since** a dog bit me when I was five years old.*
present perfect + **for** + length of time	*I've had this phobia **for** 13 years.*

We can also use adverbs such as *recently* and *always* to describe duration.

I have always been afraid of spiders.

1 Complete the sentences with the present perfect form of the words in parentheses.

1 She _____ (**be**) afraid of flying since she was a child.

2 Research _____ (**show**) that flying is one of the most common fears.

3 I _____ (**not feel**) so scared since I was little.

4 I _____ (**give**) so many talks I'm no longer scared of public speaking.

5 _____ (**you / have**) the feeling of time moving slowly when you are scared?

6 _____ (**you / see**) a doctor about your fears?

7 Studies _____ (**recently / find**) that facing your fears can help you deal with them better.

8 I _____ (**always / be**) scared of public speaking.

2 Write sentences using *for* and *since* to describe these people's fears.

1 not fly / a child
   I haven't flown since I was a child.

2 not take an elevator / five years

3 not go to the dentist / ten years old

4 not speak in public / two years

5 not touch a spider / 2000

6 not be up to the top of a tall building / the start of this year

7 not drive a car over a bridge / 2012

8 not give a presentation / a year

3 Correct the mistakes in the sentences.

1 Many people have learn fears from their parents.
2 A fear of failure have stopped many people from taking chances.
3 Studies have been done every year for 1985.
4 The research team has observed over 200 people since two years.
5 The team has interviewed 100 people for the start of March.
6 The research have had a significant impact on the understanding of fear.
7 I have been always able to stay calm by breathing slowly.

Writing skill

> When writing multiple paragraphs, it is important to organize your ideas clearly and separate different ideas into different paragraphs. You can do this when planning your writing. Think about:
>
> - dividing information into paragraphs of single topics, e.g. one paragraph for pros and one for cons, or paragraphs describing different reasons
> - selecting the best supporting details for each paragraph
> - deciding what ideas to leave out.

1 Divide the notes about fear into pros and cons. You do not need to use all the information.

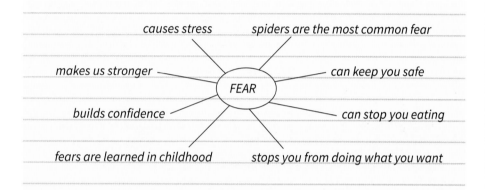

Pros	Cons

2 Based on the notes in Exercise 1, choose the best topic sentence for a paragraph on the pros of fear and the best one for a paragraph about the cons of fear.

1 Fear has both positive and negative effects.
2 Fear can have a number of negative impacts on our health.
3 Fear has a number of positives that can help to protect us from danger.
4 The positive effects of fear far outweigh the negative effects.

3 Look at the pros and cons in the table. Choose the two that best support each topic sentence.

Writing task

You are going to learn to organize your notes into paragraphs and write two paragraphs to answer the question:

"*Fear is always bad for us. Describe the pros and cons of fear.*"

Brainstorm

Use your own ideas and what you have read in *Fears, learning, coping* and *Fight or flight* to make notes about fear, when it is helpful and when it is not.

Plan

1 Organize your notes into pros and cons.

2 Choose the main topic for each paragraph.

3 Choose the best supporting details and examples to support each topic.

Write

Using your answers to the questions above, write two paragraphs on the essay question: "*Fear is always bad for us. Describe the pros and cons of fear.*" Pay attention to your use of the present perfect simple. Your text should be about 200 words long.

Share

Exchange paragraphs with a partner. Look at the checklist on page 189 and provide feedback to your partner.

Rewrite and edit

Read your partner's comments. What could you change to make your writing better? Revise your text, then check it for errors. Think about how you organized your ideas and your use of the present perfect simple.

Write the final draft.

Review

Wordlist

MACMILLAN DICTIONARY

Vocabulary preview

breathing exercises (phrase)	energy (n) ***	get over (phr v)	phobia (n)
calm (adj) **	escape (v) ***	harm (v) *	protect (v) ***
cope (v) ***	extreme (adj) **	hormone (n)	reaction (n) ***
defense (n)	face (v) ***	panic (v) *	scared (adj) **

Vocabulary development

breathe in / out	focus on	recover from	suffer from
comment on	protect (someone) from	run away from	with the help of

Academic words

adjust (v) **	encounter (v) **	injure (v) **	minimize (v) *
aware (adj) ***	external (adj) ***	internal (adj) **	response (n) ***

Academic words review

Complete the sentences with the words in the box.

adjust	dramatic	encountered	portion	response

1 One way to control your weight is to take a smaller _____ of food at mealtimes.

2 There has been a _____ rise in tourism to our country in recent years.

3 The divers _____ a large shark whilst exploring the coral reef.

4 You can _____ your seat belt by pulling on this strap.

5 The students asked the teacher for more time to revise, but they didn't get a _____.

Unit review

Reading 1	☐	I can deduce meaning from texts.
Reading 2	☐	I can understand the meaning of new words through context.
Study skill	☐	I can give and receive feedback and criticism.
Vocabulary	☐	I can use verb and preposition collocations.
Grammar	☐	I can use the present perfect simple tense.
Writing	☐	I can organize notes into paragraphs.

Discussion point

Discuss with a partner.

1 Do you prefer to read stories about invented people or real people?

2 Look at the infographic. Do real-life characters have the same qualities as hero characters in books?

3 Why are people often interested in real-life stories?

What makes a good character?

"They need to be active and make decisions about their own future."

"They overcome challenges such as fear, difficult decisions, and enemies."

"A good character needs a motivation and reason for doing something."

"We can connect with them. They remind us of ourselves or someone we know."

"They often have secrets we discover during the story."

VIDEO

AN ADVENTURER RETURNS

Before you watch

Work with your partner. Which adventure would you most like to do? Why?

1 Spend a year traveling around the world on land and in boats

2 Spend six months flying to major cities across the world

3 Spend a month walking through a major mountain range

UNIT AIMS

READING 1 Distinguishing between facts and assumptions
READING 2 Bridge sentences
STUDY SKILL Core research skills: narrow your search

VOCABULARY Expressions of time
GRAMMAR Past perfect and simple past
WRITING Linking paragraphs

Alpine rescue.

While you watch

Read the sentences and then watch the video. Complete the sentences with no more than three words or a number.

1   Erden Eruc is traveling _____.

2   He spent _____ days in his kayak to get to Cape York.

3   He was working for an _____ company when he decided to travel around the world.

4   He is raising money for a charity that helps provide basic _____ to poor communities.

After you watch

Answer the questions with a partner.

1   How do you feel about Erden's story?
    I feel inspired to do similar challenges.
    I would like to work with charities.

2   What physical challenge would you like to do?
    I would like to …

3   Do you think stories of adventure are a good way to support charities?
    They are, because …
    They aren't, because …

National hero

A Vocabulary preview

1 Complete the paragraph with the words in the box.

> continents   discovery   expedition   explorers
> hero   scientific   unexpected   unlucky

When people think of a ¹_____ they tend to think of someone doing something dangerous, such as protecting others. Very few people would think of a scientist making a ²_____ of something that saves millions of lives. However, ³_____ work has the potential to protect many more people. Scientists and ⁴_____ have traveled to many parts of the world and different ⁵_____ collecting plant samples. Often they are ⁶_____ and they don't find anything that makes a big difference. But sometimes they find something ⁷_____ that surprises them and can change lives. For example, on one ⁸_____ in Madagascar, scientists discovered a local plant, rosy periwinkle, that has since been used in medical treatments for serious conditions such as cancer. For many it was one of the most important medical discoveries of its time.

2 Discuss with a partner. Do you think a scientist is a hero? Why / why not?

B Before you read

Preparing to read

1 Read the situations below. Which people do you think are heroes?

  a A soccer player recovers from a serious injury to score the winning goal in a FIFA World Cup™ final.

  b A firefighter risks her own life to help people injured in a car crash.

  c A mountaineer climbs one of the tallest and most dangerous mountains in the world.

2 Discuss with a partner. What do you think it means to be a hero?

C Global reading

Identifying main ideas

Read *National hero* quickly and answer the questions.

1 Did Scott win the race to the South Pole?

2 Was Scott considered lucky or unlucky? Why?

3 Why is Scott considered a hero today?

National hero

1 When Robert Falcon Scott, or "Scott of the Antarctic" was reported dead, the King of England and thousands of British people attended his funeral. So why did so many people care about one explorer?

2 By the early 1900s most of the world had been discovered and recorded on maps, but the polar regions were the last unknown places to explore. Scott had planned a scientific trip in 1910, combined with an attempt to reach the South Pole on the continent of Antarctica. He hadn't planned to be in a race to be the first person to reach it. Unbeknown to him at first, a Norwegian named Roald Amundsen was trying to reach the Pole as well. Unfortunately, Scott lost the race to the Pole, and died on the journey back. His body was found in the Antarctic in a tent with some of his colleagues.

3 Britain was going through a difficult time in the early 20th century. Scott became a national hero who once again made Britain feel "great". This image of Scott remained until a publication changed people's opinions in the 1970s. The book suggested Scott and his team had made many big mistakes: they may not have had enough dogs, the men were unprepared, and they were slow at making decisions.

4 Some, however, still argue that he was an unlucky hero. Scott wanted to be the first to reach the Pole, but he also planned to conduct research, so he took a team of scientists with him. Unexpected events made the expedition into a race. Amundsen hadn't planned to go to the South Pole; his ambition was to reach the North Pole. However, in 1909 two U.S. explorers—Robert Peary and Frederick Cook—announced their two separate expeditions had reached the North Pole. Both claims are no longer accepted due to lack of proof of arrival, and the speeds they claimed were unbelievably fast. However, at the time, the claims forced Amundsen to change his plan and aim instead to be the first to reach the South Pole. Some have said that Amundsen's team were better prepared and that Scott made many mistakes. However, others believe Scott was unlucky with the weather, and he was more focused on the scientific aims of his expedition.

5 Scott's expedition brought back 40,000 scientific items, including almost 20 kilograms of rock. Of the 2,000 animal and plant species the expedition brought back, some 400 were new discoveries. The most important fossil, located next to Scott's body, was a tree from 250 million years ago. Despite running low on food, the explorers went in a different direction to enable them to find this fossil. The tree had only been found in Australia, Africa, and South America. So finding it in the Antarctic was proof that these countries and continents had all been joined together in the past. If Scott hadn't had these scientific aims, he might have been the first person to reach the South Pole, and he might have lived to tell the tale. However, it might have been much longer until we understood the important history of our planet.

GLOSSARY

fossil (n) an animal or plant, or a part of one, that lived many thousands of years ago and is kept in rock or as a piece of rock

polar regions (n) the North and South Poles

D Close reading

1 Match the names from *National hero* with the achievements.

1 Roald Amundsen ____
2 Robert Falcon Scott ____
3 Robert Peary and Frederick Cook ____

a discoveries led to the theory that the world was once a single area of land
b claimed to be the first to reach the North Pole
c first to reach the South Pole

Distinguishing between facts and assumptions

Facts are pieces of information that are definitely true. They are usually very specific and supported by proof or examples. An assumption is something that is probably true but that we cannot be certain about. It may not have examples and evidence to support it.

2 Read *National hero* again. Which of these sentences are assumptions and which are facts? How do you know? Discuss your answers with a partner.

1 Scott didn't plan to race to the South Pole.
2 Scott did not plan the trip well.
3 Robert Peary and Frederick Cook didn't reach the North Pole.
4 The failure of Scott's expedition was due to bad luck.
5 Scott's expedition brought back many items for scientists to study.
6 Scott's scientific aims stopped him being the first to the South Pole.

3 Find the details that support the facts in Exercise 2.

E Critical thinking

1 Do you agree that Scott was a hero? Why / why not?

Scott was probably considered a hero because …
I disagree. I don't think he was a hero because …

2 Why do you think the expedition and its discoveries were thought to be so important?

The expedition was probably so important because …

Study skills | Core research skills: narrow your search

To narrow your search to more relevant items, include more key words in your 'search string' and choose your search string with care.

- Which words best describe what you're looking for? Which are most likely to be used as words for making electronic links?
- Consider synonyms.
- Might unrelated subjects share key words with your topic? If so, use at least one word that applies only to your topic.
- Which specific areas of your topic do you need to focus on? Which words identify these?
- If a search string proves particularly useful, note it down for future use.

© Stella Cottrell (2013)

GLOSSARY

search string (n) the words and numbers you use in an Internet search

1   Look at these different sources you can use for research. Discuss with a partner the strengths and weaknesses of each source.

> academic articles   books   newspapers   the Internet

2   Read *Core research skills: narrow your search*. Then organize the words in the box below from best to worst for an Internet search about famous explorers.

> adventure   dangerous   discover   expedition
> explorer   famous   find   people   travel

3   Compare your answers with a partner. Which other words would be good to use in your search?

4   Try entering different combinations of your search words into your tablet, laptop, or phone. Which ones do you think find the most interesting and useful information?

5   Make notes about one of the explorers using your own words.

The power of the written word

A Vocabulary preview

1 Match the words in bold with the correct definitions.

1	**alphabet** (n)	a	a long written story, usually about people and events that aren't real
2	**by hand** (phrase)		
3	**entertain** (v)	b	a set of letters in a particular order that are used for writing a language
4	**equipment** (n)		
5	**inform** (v)	c	the items or machines that you need to do a particular job
6	**novel** (n)	d	using your hands rather than a machine
7	**print** (v)	e	to give someone information about something
8	**the written word** (phrase)	f	to make books, newspapers, or magazines
		g	involving writing in general
		h	to do something for people to enjoy and have fun

2 Complete the sentences with words from Exercise 1.

1 _____ is more powerful today than the spoken word.

2 My computer is the most important piece of _____ I need to work.

3 We don't need to _____ books anymore because we can read everything online.

4 Products produced _____ are better than ones made by machine.

5 Children find it easier to learn the _____ for a new language than adults.

6 Books should only be written and read to _____ and educate.

7 A _____ can tell us many things about a period in history or a particular culture.

8 We need to read stories to children so we can teach them as well as _____ them.

3 Check (✓) the opinions you agree with in Exercise 2. Compare your choices with a partner.

B Before you read

Preparing to read

Work with a partner. Discuss these questions.

1 Why do you think writing is important in different cultures?

2 How do you think the way we write has changed over time?

1 Human communication has developed from a completely spoken form to a wide variety of writing styles and ways of producing texts. Originally this would have been just simple signs and symbols; however we are now able to send a huge number of messages, at the same time, to thousands of people across the world.

2 One of the earliest forms of communication to have moved beyond simple pictures was the hieroglyphics system developed by the ancient Egyptians. This writing system was a mixture of symbols and images. It was not a language in the way we understand today but it was certainly a way of communicating. The first written language with what we would recognize as an alphabet came from the Phoenicians—an ancient civilization based around the eastern Mediterranean Sea. The alphabet had 22 letters. There were no vowels—all the letters were consonants.

3 As time passed, and people moved further around the world, so their alphabets changed with them. Different cultures also added more letters to represent the different sounds of their own language. For many, writing has even developed into an art form known as calligraphy and is an important part of the culture in a lot of places, including parts of East Asia and the Middle East. Arabic calligraphy can be seen across many public sites from fountains to schools.

4 Although alphabets and writing had started to grow and take on new forms, there was one other major problem. There was no good-quality product to write on. Chinese inventor Ts'ai Lun created paper in the year CE 105. Up until then, people wrote on a wide range of items, including animal skins, plants, and cloth. Even after paper had been invented, it took a long time to become the main way of keeping written records. Paper-making was next introduced to Korea and Japan, but it took nearly another 500 years to reach other parts of the world.

5 An additional challenge, besides developing a material to write on, was that it was difficult to produce copies of texts. Before the invention of the printing press, when something needed to be copied it had to be done by hand. People who had a good education were paid to copy complete books page by page. Around 600 years ago, there was a significant increase to the speed of this process due to the invention of the printing press. These machines needed several people to make them work and they could only print a few thousand pages a day. They were also the size of a room. This press, however, was perhaps one of the most important inventions because it gave more power and opportunities to ordinary people.

GLOSSARY

printing press (n) a machine used for making newspapers, books, and magazines

6　While only companies could print texts, the printing press meant more people had access to the materials that helped them to read and write, which meant they had a better education and felt more powerful. Arguably, this led to the beginning of mass communication. The results of this communication revolution can be seen in stories and novels. Previously, writing was mainly used to inform people and share ideas about life, but the printing press changed this as more and more books were written to entertain people. At first, many stories took the form of a long poem or a play. Plays, such as Shakespeare's, became forms of entertainment. Stories were then divided into chapters in the form of novels. *Don Quixote* by the Spanish writer Miguel de Cervantes is considered by many as the first modern novel and multiple editions have been produced around the world.

7　Unfortunately, one thing holding back the growth of the written word was that the writing equipment did not develop quickly. In Europe, for nearly a thousand years, people used quills—bird feathers—which were difficult to write with. This did not improve much until 1822, when John Mitchell set up a pen factory in Birmingham, England. These pens contained steel and stayed sharp for longer but they were not very good at writing on many surfaces. The first ballpoint pen design was submitted by John J. Loud. This original ballpoint pen was only invented around a century ago, and it took another 50 years to look like today's pens.

8　Clearly, the development of writing did not stop with the development of better pens and printing methods. The invention of computers, tablets, and smartphones has changed the way we read, write, and learn. Practically a new language has been developed due to the increased use of short forms for texts and social media communication. Some also argue that the use of images and emojis has also made communication today more like cave paintings or hieroglyphics of ancient times. Self-publishing in a digital form has meant that more and more people can publish their own novels. The Internet has also meant that fewer and fewer students are using libraries to research topics. Even just 25 years ago most essays would have been written by hand. From the words and symbols we use, to the processes of cutting, pasting, and deleting to start again, what we write and how we write it has changed completely.

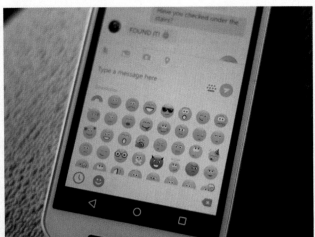

C Global reading

> Bridge sentences are sometimes used to connect the previous paragraph with the one to come. When this occurs, the bridge sentence is the first sentence in a paragraph and the topic sentence appears after it. The bridge sentence usually repeats ideas from the previous paragraph in different words.

1 Skim *The power of the written word* and identify the paragraphs that start with bridge sentences. What are the bridge sentences?

2 Find the topic sentences in paragraphs 2–8 and match the paragraphs with the main ideas.

Paragraph 2 ____   a Changing use of alphabets

Paragraph 3 ____   b Copying and producing texts

Paragraph 4 ____   c Inventing a good writing material

Paragraph 5 ____   d The creation of writing equipment and pens

Paragraph 6 ____   e Technology's effect on writing

Paragraph 7 ____   f The first writing systems

Paragraph 8 ____   g Beginning to communicate with many people

D Close reading

Read *The power of the written word* again and answer the questions, using supporting details in the paragraphs.

1 What was the first written communication after basic pictures?

2 Where in public can we see calligraphy?

3 What things other than animal skins did people write on?

4 Which two countries learned to make paper after China?

5 Who copied books before the printing press?

6 How big was a printing press?

7 What two types of storytelling and entertainment were popular before the novel?

8 Who invented the first ballpoint pen?

9 What part of communication today do people think is like cave paintings or hieroglyphics?

E Critical thinking

1 How many inventions can you identify in the reading text? With a partner rank the importance of each invention in changing how we communicate.

2 Can you think of any other events or inventions that have changed how we communicate?

Vocabulary development

Adverbs and adverbial phrases of time

1 Complete the sentences with the words and phrases in the box.

> as soon as   by the early   constantly   eventually
> not until   previously   recently   shortly after

1 _____ 20th century, a lot of railroads had been built in the U.K.

2 Someone else made the journey _____ her first expedition.

3 _____, after a lot of failed attempts, Edison invented the light bulb.

4 Everyone changes their smartphone straight away _____ a new model is released.

5 _____ the discovery of fossil fuels did people do so much damage to the planet.

6 Technology is _____ changing and improving.

7 _____, the fax machine and letters were the main written communication, but now they are rarely used.

8 _____, just in the last few months, scientists have discovered new ways to fight some major diseases.

2 Which words and phrases from Exercise 1 are used with a specific time or event and which ones can be used with an unspecified point in time? Put the words and phrases in the correct column.

Specified time or event	Unspecified time
by the early 20th century	eventually

3 Think about important events in your country. Use words and phrases from Exercise 1 to tell your partner about the effect of these.

The printing press had a big impact. Previously, all books had to be copied by hand.

Academic words

1 Match the words in bold with the correct definitions.

1	**chapter** (n)	a	an opinion that people have about someone or something, which may not be true
2	**conduct** (v)		
3	**edition** (n)	b	a set of copies of a book published at the same time. A new version will be different to the old version
4	**enable** (v)		
5	**image** (n)	c	a magazine, newspaper, or book
6	**locate** (v)	d	to find the exact place where someone or something is
7	**publication** (n)	e	to do something in an organized way
8	**revolution** (n)	f	a sudden or major change, especially in ideas or methods
		g	to give someone the ability or opportunity to do something
		h	one of the sections of a book that usually has a number and a title

2 Complete the sentences with words from Exercise 1.

1 I loved the book as soon as I read the first _____.

2 The new _____ of the book contained new research that wasn't in the first.

3 The invention of the Internet was the biggest modern _____ in how we live and work.

4 They frequently _____ research to see how people use technology.

5 A popular _____, like a well-known magazine, can have a lot of influence over a society.

6 He gives the _____ of being calm and confident, but he is actually very nervous.

7 They managed to _____ the island after many months of searching.

8 Learning to read will _____ people to have many more opportunities in life.

3 Discuss these questions with a partner.

1 Think of something that has influenced you a lot. How did it influence you and why? Think about:

   a chapter of a book   a publication   an image of someone

2 What invention enabled the greatest revolution in sharing information?

Writing model

You are going to learn the difference between the past perfect and simple past and how to link paragraphs in an essay. You are then going to use these skills to write the story of an important invention or discovery that changed the world.

A Model

Read the model and use the information to complete the table below.

Like many other inventions, the microwave was based on technology that people had previously used for other purposes. The ability of microwaves to conduct heat was accidently discovered by Percy Spencer. He had been working with radars when he found that the heat from them melted the candy bar in his pocket. From this he discovered that microwaves could be used to cook food. His company had registered the idea by 1945, but they didn't sell microwaves to the public until early 1947. At first, microwaves were very big and expensive, but they went on to create a revolution in the kitchen.

As soon as microwaves became cheaper and smaller it meant more people could buy them. Today microwaves are very common and easy to locate, but some people have been concerned about the health impact of microwaves. As soon as microwaves had been built and sold cheaply there was a sharp rise in the number of processed meals available. Eating enough of these will eventually have a negative impact on your health. However, cooking fresh foods such as vegetables in a microwave is as healthy as any other cooking method and much faster.

B Analyze

Invention / discovery	How	Effect
compass	by the Chinese using a natural magnet between the 9th and 11th century CE	increased trade and helped people to explore more countries
telephone	1876 by Alexander Graham Bell. Used existing technology	made communication much faster
microwave		

Read the model and the Analyze table again and answer the questions with a partner.

1 Why was the microwave an important invention?
2 Which invention in the table do you think was the most important? Why?

Grammar

Past perfect and simple past

Use the **past perfect** to talk about an action in the past that was completed before another action in the past. The **simple past** is used to talk about a past habit, event, and state.

heat **had touched** the candy bar *(earlier past moment)*	the candy bar **melted** *(past moment)*	today

Form	Examples
Past perfect	
had / hadn't + past participle	*alphabets and writing **had started** to grow* *Amundsen **hadn't planned** to go to the South Pole.*
Simple past	
subject + verb + **-ed**	*From this he **discovered** that microwaves could be used to cook food.*
subject + **did not (didn't)** + base form	*they **didn't sell** microwaves to the public until early 1947.*
Irregular verbs do not follow a pattern. You have to memorize them.	*fall* → **fell**

1 Complete the sentences using the past perfect form of the verbs in parentheses.

1 Before the invention of the telephone, people _____ (communicate) largely by letter.

2 They _____ (realize) the importance of their invention until it changed the way people communicated.

3 Tim Berners-Lee created the World Wide Web in 1989. However, the writer Arthur C. Clarke _____ (predict) a similar idea in the 1970s.

4 It _____ (take) days to travel across the country.

5 Percy Spencer discovered the microwave when he realized his machine _____ (cook) the food in his pocket.

6 The company _____ (sell) over a million by the end of the decade.

2 Choose the correct option to complete each sentence.

1 In 1988, no one **heard / had heard** of the Internet. Twenty years later billions of people **used / had used** it.

2 Before the invention of e-mail, people **waited / had waited** days for letters to arrive.

3 In 1950, 80% of Britons **had not had / didn't have** a car, but by 2000 80% **had / had had** a car.

4 In 2015, people **sent / had sent** 16 million texts per minute. No one **had ever sent / sent** a text message before 1992.

5 The invention of the airplane **had made / made** it much quicker to travel around the world.

3 Complete the sentences with the appropriate form of the past perfect or simple past.

1 I _____ (hear) of a video player until my grandfather showed me one.

2 When my grandfather was a child most people _____ (have) a television.

3 My father _____ (use) a computer by the time he was 20 years old. I used one much younger, at three years old.

4 I opened my e-mail account in 2014. Before that I _____ (send) a message to anyone.

5 When the company _____ (start), the owners _____ (invent) two new products.

6 Before 2006 no one _____ (use) the website. Now hundreds of people visit it every day.

4 Write about these situations in either the simple past or past perfect and the words in parentheses.

1 You went on vacation with your friend. It was her first flight.
(**friend / never / fly**) _____

2 Your grandfather got his first smartphone for his birthday.
(**not / use / birthday**) _____

3 There was a new IT system. After two weeks, everyone could use it.
(**everyone / able to use / two weeks**) _____

4 She didn't see many wild animals. Then she went to South Africa.
(**see / until / South Africa**) _____

Writing skill

When writing an essay it is important to link your paragraphs to each other, to the essay question, and to the main idea in your introduction. Each paragraph should have one main idea and the paragraphs should be well connected. You can do this by using:

Topic sentences

Usually the first or second sentence of a paragraph. The topic sentence contains the main idea of a paragraph.

Bridge sentences

Usually the first sentence of a paragraph. This connects one paragraph to the previous one by repeating the main idea.

Concluding sentences

The last sentence or second last sentence in a paragraph. These summarize the main idea of a paragraph.

Linking paragraphs

1 Look back at the two paragraphs on page 146. Underline the topic sentences, draw a box around the concluding sentences, and circle the bridge sentence.

2 Use sentences a–e to complete the paragraphs.

   ^{1}___ The British scientist had graduated from Oxford University before he started working in Switzerland. Berners-Lee had noticed that the scientists working there had problems sharing information. He used existing technology and new technology to create the World Wide Web. ^{2}___

   ^{3}___ ^{4}___ The Web has changed how people study and learn and opened opportunities for many people. Many businesses have been launched and become some of the biggest on the planet. ^{5}___

   a As a result of this decision, the world was given a revolution in work, communication, and shopping.

   b Tim Berners-Lee invented the World Wide Web in 1989.

   c Instead of making money from this new and significant invention, he and his colleagues gave the technology away for free.

   d Arguably, the Web has changed work, life, and communication like no other invention before.

   e Many believe it was the most important invention of the 20th century.

3 Think of one important invention or discovery. Write two topic sentences:

   1 Describe the invention or discovery.
   2 Describe why it was important.

4 Think about your content of the paragraphs. Write one bridge sentence to connect the two paragraphs.

Writing task

Write the story of an important invention or discovery that changed the world. Explain how it was made and why it was important.

Brainstorm and plan

1   Decide on the invention or discovery you want to focus on.

2   If you can, research how and when the invention or discovery was made. Remember to use your core research skills from page 139.

3   Complete the table below.

Discovery	How / when	Effect

Write

Using your ideas and research above, write two paragraphs on the invention or discovery. Pay attention to your connecting sentences. Pay attention to your use of the past perfect and simple past. Your text should be 150 to 200 words long.

Share

Exchange paragraphs with a partner. Look at the checklist on page 189 and provide feedback to your partner.

Rewrite and edit

Read your partner's comments. What could you change to make your writing better? Revise your text, then check it for errors. Think about:

- the links between the paragraphs
- linking back to the essay question
- your use of past perfect and simple past.

Write the final draft.

Review

Wordlist

MACMILLAN DICTIONARY

Vocabulary preview

alphabet (n) *	entertain (v) **	hero (n) **	scientific (adj) ***
by hand (phrase)	equipment (n) ***	inform (v) ***	the written word (phrase)
continent (n) **	expedition (n) **	novel (n) ***	unexpected (adj) **
discovery (n) ***	explorer (n)	print (v) ***	unlucky (adj)

Vocabulary development

as soon as (phrase)	constantly (adv) **	not until (phrase)	recently (adv) ***
by the early (phrase)	eventually (adv) ***	previously (adv) ***	shortly after (phrase)

Academic words

chapter (n) ***	edition (n) **	image (n) ***	publication (n) ***
conduct (v) ***	enable (v) ***	locate (v) **	revolution (n) ***

Academic words review

Complete the sentences with the words in the box.

conduct   edition   image   injured   publication

1 There is a new _____ of *Understanding Economics*. It has just been published.
2 Ahmed is going to _____ a survey into what students think of the new menus in the canteen.
3 Companies worry about their corporate _____ and how the public perceives them.
4 Andy fell during the soccer game and _____ his left arm.
5 *Kite Surfing Today* is a brand new _____ for enthusiasts of this exciting sport. Be sure to get a copy!

Unit review

Reading 1		I can distinguish between specific facts and assumptions.
Reading 2		I can use bridge sentences to navigate a text.
Study skill		I can use core research to narrow Internet searches.
Vocabulary		I can use expressions of time to describe when something happened.
Grammar		I can use the past perfect and simple past.
Writing		I can link paragraphs together and back to main ideas and the essay question.

Discussion point

Discuss with a partner.

1 Which environmental problem in the infographic do you think is the biggest concern?

2 Which solution do you think is the most effective?

3 Why do you think it is important to protect the environment?

ENVIRONMENTAL PROBLEMS

Areas of rainforests the size of about 30 to 50 soccer fields are cut down every minute.

Plastic pollution affects hundreds of plants and animals in the sea.

Many people live in areas with not enough water and this number is likely to increase.

A lot of the food in the world is wasted but at the same time millions are dying of hunger.

ENVIRONMENTAL SOLUTIONS

If all newspapers in the world were recycled, we could save approximately 250 million trees each year.

In the U.K., large stores charge money for plastic bags.

About 70% of all fresh water used is used in farming. Reducing food waste may reduce the amount of water used.

In some countries, such as France, supermarkets must give food waste to charity.

VIDEO

COMING HOME TO NEST

Before you watch

Answer the questions with a partner.

1 Are there any animals that are protected in your country? How are they protected?

2 Do any animals travel to your country to have their young? Which animals and where does this happen?

UNIT AIMS

READING 1 Scanning for examples: phrases to introduce examples
READING 2 Scanning for examples: groups of three
STUDY SKILL Creative problem solving: identify a strategy

VOCABULARY Words to describe environmental issues
GRAMMAR Passives: present and past perfect
WRITING Summarizing arguments in a conclusion

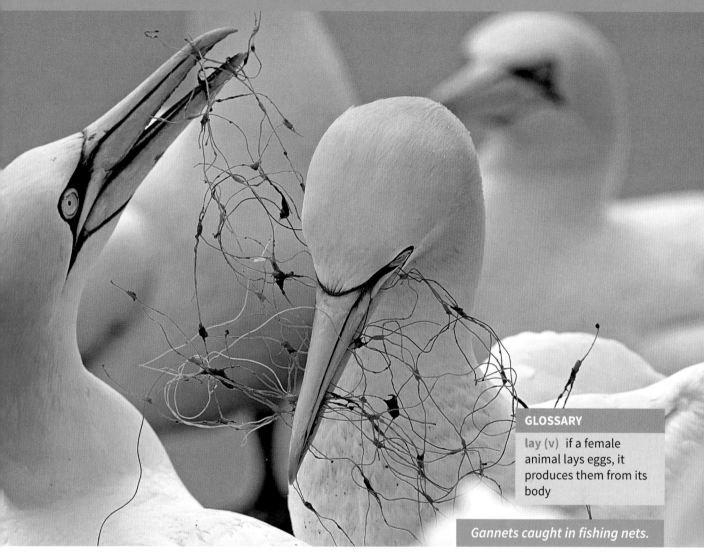

GLOSSARY

lay (v) if a female animal lays eggs, it produces them from its body

Gannets caught in fishing nets.

While you watch

Read the information and then watch the video. Match each number with a piece of information.

1 25 to 30 ____
2 15 ____
3 100 million ____
4 1 million ____
5 15 million ____

a Age at which a female returns to the beach it was born on
b Number of years turtles have existed
c Number of eggs laid on the beach each year
d Length in kilometers of the beach
e Number of turtles killed every year in the 1960s

After you watch

Answer the questions with a partner.

1 How have local farming and fishing methods changed in your country?

   They have changed by …

2 Do you think people are more or less concerned about the environment nowadays than in the past?

   Yes, because …   No, because …

3 Would you like to be involved in an environmental charity?

   Yes, because …   No, because …

Rainforests of the sea

A Vocabulary preview

Complete the sentences with the words in the box.

| coast | damage | ecosystem | fish | forecast | ocean | oil spill | tropical |

1 Pollution is likely to have a serious effect on the local _____.

2 The _____ around the edge of the island has been affected by the development of the tourist industry.

3 An _____ from a boat can kill hundreds of birds and sea life for miles around.

4 Cars _____ the environment and are causing an increase in global temperatures.

5 In many places there are limits on the areas people are allowed to _____. Each country can only catch a certain amount.

6 Increased human demand has caused low fish numbers in some parts of the _____.

7 Scientists _____ a temperature rise of up to ten degrees over the next 100 years.

8 Fiji is a beautiful, hot country that consists of 332 _____ islands.

B Before you read

Activating prior knowledge

1 Read the glossary and heading, and look at the image. Why do you think coral reefs are called "rainforests of the sea"?

2 Skim the text to check your predictions.

C Global reading

Summarizing main ideas

Read *Rainforests of the sea*. Do the statements match the writer's claims? Write:
Y (Yes) if the statement matches the claims of the writer
N (No) if the statement contradicts the claims of the writer
NG (Not Given) if it is impossible to say what the writer thinks about this.

1 Coral reefs are important for tourism. _____

2 Tourists in the sea have a large effect on the coral. _____

3 Hundreds of species have become extinct due to coral damage. _____

4 Pollution causes algae to grow and affects the water quality. _____

5 Damage to coral reefs causes problems for many other animals. _____

6 Coral reefs are forecast to be completely destroyed in the next 50 years. _____

Rainforests of the sea

1   Coral reefs, sometimes called the rainforests of the sea, make up only 0.1% of the ocean floor, but they are home to a quarter of the world's fish. Reefs grow in tropical waters. The largest is Australia's Great Barrier Reef, which is over 1,200 miles long off the Queensland coast. Reefs are not only important for food; they are also valuable for tourism. For example, Florida's reef is worth about $6.3 billion every year in tourism. Unfortunately, the consequences of increased human activity are damaging reefs around the world.

2   Tourism has had an effect on coral reefs but it is often connected with a wider range of issues. In areas such as the Caribbean, where tourism is connected with the beaches and the sea, tourism can have a number of effects. Activities like snorkeling and diving, as well as oil spills from boats, can damage reefs. But this effect is quite small compared to the effect of building resorts and ports. In some areas, a large percentage of the waste and dirty water from hotels also goes into coastal waters directly. This allows algae to grow faster and damage the coral.

3   Coral reefs need clean, clear water to live. However, with developments along the coast, from the tourist industry to other traditional trades, reefs are damaged in a lot of ways. Disposal of pollutants into the water means they cover coral reefs. This can make harmful plants, such as algae, grow faster and lower water quality. Pollution can also increase the risk of disease and slow coral growth. This pollution can come from thousands of miles away. For instance, pollution from Mississippi or Mexico can affect the reefs in Florida.

4   On an even wider scale, global warming and sea temperatures are affecting wildlife throughout the world's oceans and in particular coral reefs. Due to climate change, ocean temperatures have been increasing and they are forecast to continue to increase. The increased carbon dioxide is being taken in by the sea. This has raised the levels of acid in the sea, the temperature, and sea levels, which can result in coral bleaching. Since coral reefs provide food for other animals, this then affects the entire ecosystem.

5   Coral reefs provide wide opportunities for fishing and so offer food for over a billion people. This means they also support the economy of many communities. The effect of overfishing on coral reef areas can lead to fewer important reef species in many locations. Such problems can then affect the whole environment and local businesses, which rely on those fish. A bigger population and the increased demand for food has meant many areas have been damaged or destroyed completely by overfishing.

6   Unfortunately, there is not one easy solution to solve such a problem as it is connected to protecting the world's environment as a whole. Every positive change, such as using less water and riding a bike instead of driving a car, to planting trees and throwing your trash away responsibly, can arguably help to protect some of the most beautiful ecosystems in the world.

GLOSSARY

algae (n) plants that have no roots, stems, or leaves and grow in water or in other wet places

bleaching (n) a loss of color in corals which may eventually cause them to die

coral reef (n) a hard natural structure under the sea that is formed from coral

pollutants (n) things that cause pollution

trash (n) rubbish such as paper and plastic bags

D Close reading

1 Read *Rainforests of the sea* again and answer the questions.

1 What is worse for coral reefs—snorkeling and diving or building resorts?

2 What do pollutants encourage to grow?

3 What causes coral bleaching?

Scanning for examples 1

> **Phrases to introduce examples**
>
> Examples are given to help explain and support a main idea. Examples can often be found by locating key phrases that introduce them, e.g.
>
> *For example / Another example is*
>
> *such as*
>
> *For instance*

2 Find the examples in the text for each of these points.

1 A reef that is valuable for tourism _____

2 A location where tourism is based around the coast _____

3 Two locations that can affect the coral in Florida _____

4 Something being lost that affects local businesses _____

5 Four things you can do to protect coral reefs

_____

_____

_____

_____

E Critical thinking

1 Work with a partner. Which thing from the text do you think has the biggest negative effect on the oceans as a whole?

I think … has the biggest effect because …

2 What other issues do you know that affect the world's seas and oceans?

… has a big effect on the ocean because …

Study skills — Creative problem solving: identify a strategy

For your subject, there will be common ways that could be applied to the kind of problem you have been set. If you identify the type of problem correctly, this generally gives you an idea about the steps needed to arrive at the solution.

Weigh up alternative approaches

Note down a list of strategies that might, potentially, lead to a solution to the problem. Give initial thought to where each might lead.

What are the advantages of each solution or combination of solutions? What might be the disadvantages?

© Stella Cottrell (2013)

1 Read *Creative problem solving: identify a strategy* then look at the problem and solution below. What are the advantages and disadvantages of the solution?

Problem: Plastic bottles are difficult to recycle and take a long time to break down.

Solution: Ban plastic bottles.

2 Work in small groups. Choose one problem below and think of four different solutions.

1 Cars cause air pollution.

2 Animals are dying because people are destroying where they live.

3 Compare all of your solutions using the table. When you compare each one write the letter of the stronger solution in each box.

	Solution B	Solution C	Solution D
Solution A			
Solution B			
Solution C			

4 Choose the best solution to the problem.

Living together

A Vocabulary preview

1 Match the words in bold with the correct definitions.

1	**attack** (v)	a	to kill animals for food or for their skin or other parts, or for sport
2	**endangered** (adj)	b	describing an animal or plant that may soon disappear from the world
3	**hunt** (v)		
4	**law** (n)	c	an area of land that is protected so that people cannot harm the animals and plants that live there
5	**livestock** (n)		
6	**nature reserve** (n)	d	a set of rules that people must obey
7	**species** (n)	e	the activities of buying and selling goods or services
8	**trade** (n)	f	to hurt a person, animal, or place in a violent way
		g	a plant or animal group
		h	animals such as cows, sheep, and pigs that are kept on farms

2 Complete the sentences with words from Exercise 1 in the correct form.

1 People should not be allowed to _____ animals for fun.

2 _____ in endangered animals should be banned.

3 It's a good idea to charge tourists to visit _____ and see the animals.

4 Wild animals only usually _____ farm animals because people have killed too many wild animals for food.

5 It is important that a lot of different _____ can live in one ecosystem.

6 People keep too much _____ for food. We need to eat less meat.

7 It should be against the _____ to build on land that is home to wildlife.

8 _____ animals do not need to be protected. It is natural that not all animals live forever.

3 Check (✓) the sentences you agree with in Exercise 2. Compare and discuss your choices with a partner.

B Before you read

Activating prior knowledge

Discuss these questions with a partner.

1 Why do you think we see more animals in cities and near our homes today than we did in the past?

2 What problems do you think exist between humans and animals today?

LIVING *TOGETHER*

1 The development of farming, access to clean water, and better medical care have seen the human population thrive like no other species. Some forecasts suggest that the human population could reach nearly 10 billion by 2050. People are likely to compete with animals for space more than ever as we increase the food supply to feed more people. Methods such as giving more land to farming, using harmful chemicals, and transporting food around the world are likely to continue to damage a variety of ecosystems. Hunting and damage to habitats where animals live continue to threaten animal numbers as well. While we are likely to always compete, many organizations and governments are implementing plans to help deal with this crisis. From protecting individual species and areas of land to planting new forests across entire regions, there is hope for the future.

2 In the 1960s just one in five people lived in cities in China. Today, approximately half of the Chinese population lives in a city. At the same time, the number of people has more than doubled, with one in seven people in the world living in China. This has caused problems for the environment in the country. Increasing demands for food have led to a lot of land being damaged and at risk of turning to desert as it is farmed too much. This has led to an increased risk of damaging weather, including floods, not enough water, and dust storms. It has also affected the natural habitats of some plants and animals. In order to restore the natural environments, new forests are being planted to cover an area just under the size of Spain.

3 Arguably, planting more trees is something that could be attempted in almost any country. One solution that has been introduced throughout the world is nature reserves. These are not a new idea with the first protected area for wildlife being created in Sri Lanka in the 3rd century BCE. However, their increase and success has been huge. The first major nature reserve, as we know today, was started in 1872 with the Yellowstone National Park in the U.S. Today, wildlife reserves cover 14 million km²—an area the size of China and India together. While these have been crucial in protecting animals, some argue that this area eventually needs to increase to near 20% to stop further extinctions.

> **GLOSSARY**
>
> **extinction (n)** a situation where an animal or plant of one species is no longer alive
>
> **habitat (n)** the area an animal or plant lives in

4 Kenya is one country known for its nature reserves. However, it still faces many challenges in working alongside local communities to protect wildlife. In the past, the local Maasai men hunted lions. Part of the tradition of becoming a man was to hunt and kill a lion. Lions were also hunted because of attacks on the local community's farm animals. Now former lion hunters are some of the main protectors of these great animals. Using traditional knowledge of being able to find lions and modern GPS technology, they are able to easily follow and find the animals, so they know how to protect them. In addition to finding and supporting the lions, the technology is also used for other things such as to find lost farm animals, other endangered animals, and even lost local children. Communities now work with the former hunters so that people, farm animals, and the lions are kept safe. Therefore, the population of lions has increased in recent years.

5 Many animals have been hunted to extinction or close to extinction in the last hundred years. Species of wolf, leopard, and bear have all disappeared from some countries. Often animals have been hunted to protect farm animals from attack but in some cases, such as with rhinos and elephants, it can be because they are considered extremely valuable. In recent years, some animals such as the southern white rhino, the American bison, and the bald eagle have been protected from decline by different groups and organizations. Under the right circumstances, protection efforts have been very successful. Numbers of southern white rhinos had fallen to around 50 at the start of the 20th century but increased to about 20,000 in recent years. This increase happened largely because rhinos from a small population in a reserve in South Africa were secretly moved to other parts of the continent. They were then protected and their populations were able to grow.

6 Hunting is, however, still one of the biggest threats to many different species, including rhinos. The black rhino and other animals are seriously endangered due to the illegal wildlife trade, where animal parts or live animals are sold around the world even though it is against the law. A number of different solutions have been suggested. These include educating people to stop the demand for wildlife, giving more authority and power to the rangers who protect animals, and even changes in laws. There is a lot of debate about which areas of hunting and trade should be made legal or prohibited and whether changes in laws around hunting could help wildlife or increase demand and make the problem worse. At the moment, no solution has been found and it could take several different ideas to help protect endangered species from human threats.

GLOSSARY

ranger (n) someone whose job is to protect wildlife or a nature reserve

C Global reading

Match the problems in *Living together* with the solutions.

1 Too much farming damaging land ___
2 Needing a solution that works around the world ___
3 Lions being killed ___
4 Species hunted until they disappear ___

a GPS and support from the community
b Increase in nature reserves
c Protection from groups and organizations
d Planting more trees

D Close reading

Groups of three

As well as scanning for phrases to introduce examples, you can sometimes find different examples listed together in groups. In order to make the writing brief and clear, authors often list examples in groups of three. For example:

Coral reefs are damaged by a number of different factors, including <u>pollution</u>, <u>tourist activities</u>, and <u>increased sea temperatures</u>.

Read *Living together* again and find three examples for each of the following:

1 Methods needed to increase food supply
2 Damaging weather as land turns to desert
3 Things, other than lions, that GPS technology has been used to find
4 Species that have disappeared from some countries
5 Animals protected by organizations and groups
6 Possible solutions to the illegal wildlife trade

E Critical thinking

1 Which solutions in the text do you think would be the most effective for the problems below? Why?

1 Damage to coral reefs and ocean pollution
2 Air pollution in cities
3 Animals appearing in cities and people's homes

2 Think about conservation issues in your own country. What solutions do you think would be effective?

Doing ... would work because ...

Vocabulary development

Words to describe environmental issues

1 Match the words in bold with the correct definitions.

1	**carbon footprint** (n)	a	the cutting down of large areas of trees
2	**climate change** (n)	b	to change from a solid substance into a liquid
3	**deforestation** (n)	c	too many people living in one area
4	**fossil fuels** (n)	d	the differences that are thought to be affecting the world's weather so that it is becoming warmer
5	**global warming** (n)		
6	**melt** (v)	e	the slow increase in the temperature of the Earth caused partly by pollution
7	**overfishing** (n)		
8	**overpopulation** (n)	f	the amount of carbon dioxide a person, organization, building, etc. produces
		g	the damage to a river or an area of sea caused by catching too many fish
		h	fuels such as coal or oil

2 Complete the sentences with words from Exercise 1.

1 Demand for homes, food, and materials has led to increased _____.

2 Many countries are trying to reduce the amount of _____ they use.

3 _____ is causing the polar ice to _____ and sea levels to rise.

4 _____ means we do not have enough resources to provide food and water for everyone.

5 Our _____ has increased significantly as we consume more and use polluting technology more.

6 _____ has endangered many species of ocean life.

7 _____ is the biggest environmental issue faced by humanity.

3 Think about the problems in Exercises 1 and 2. Discuss these questions with a partner.

1 Which problem(s) do you think are most serious?

2 Which problem(s) most affect your country?

3 What is being done to solve these problems in your country?

Academic words

1 Match the words in bold with the correct definitions.

1	**authority** (n)	a	facts or conditions that affect a situation
2	**circumstances** (n)	b	very important
3	**conclusion** (n)	c	the process of getting rid of something
4	**consequence** (n)	d	something that you decide is true after thinking about it carefully and looking at all the evidence
5	**crucial** (adj)		
6	**disposal** (n)	e	to officially stop something being done
7	**legal** (adj)	f	relating to the law
8	**prohibit** (v)	g	a result or effect of something
		h	the power to make decisions or tell people what to do

2 Complete the questions with words from Exercise 1.

1 Do you think we should _____ the use of fossil fuels to protect the environment?

2 Some people have drawn the _____ that climate change is not real. Do you agree?

3 Do you think governments should have the _____ to limit the number of flights we take?

4 What do you think will be the _____ of using fossil fuels?

5 Should we ban the _____ of waste at sea?

6 What is the most _____ change we need to make to protect the environment?

7 Under what _____ would you give up your car?

8 In most countries it is _____ to own as many cars as you want. Do you think this law should be changed?

3 Discuss the questions in Exercise 2 in groups. Are these effective solutions to the following environmental problems?

1 Water pollution
2 Overpopulation in cities
3 Global warming

Writing model

You are going to learn about using present and past perfect passive and how to summarize arguments in a conclusion. You are then going to use these to write the conclusion to an essay that answers the following question:
"*Describe an environmental problem in your country and suggest ways to resolve it*".

A Analyze

Look at the brainstorm below. What do you think would be the most effective way to solve the issue? Read the model and check your answer.

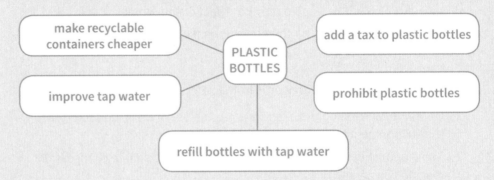

B Model

In conclusion, producing plastic bottles uses a lot of fuel that contributes to global warming. This essay has presented a number of effective solutions to dealing with the crucial issue of too many plastic bottles such as using other products, having the authority to tax bottles, and possibly prohibiting their use. The last solution is probably the most effective; however it is also the hardest to implement. Arguably, the other two solutions could work well together. Adding a tax to plastic bottles will make them more expensive. This will then encourage people to look for the cheaper products that can be recycled and therefore lower their carbon footprint.

1 What do you think the main argument of the author was in the introduction? What do you think each paragraph covered?

2 Discuss these questions with a partner.

　1 What are the three main environmental problems affecting your region?

　2 How can these be solved?

　3 What are the strengths and weaknesses of these solutions?

Grammar

The passive: present and past perfect

We use the passive:

1 to summarize and conclude essays and information

   *A number of solutions **have been presented** …*

2 when we do not need to know who did an action or when it is obvious who did the action

   *Fewer animals **have been hunted**.*

3 when the action or the object is more important than the person who did the action.

   *The lions **have been protected** by local people.*

   Notice we use ***by*** to introduce the person doing the action.

   *New regulations have been created **by** the WWF.*

Present perfect passive

Form: *have / has[n't]* + *been* + past participle

*Only 1% of tropical plants **have been tested** for medical use.*

Use: We use the **present perfect passive** to talk about events that happened at an unspecified point in time, or to connect the past with the present.

Past perfect passive

Form: *had[n't]* + *been* + past participle

*The American bison **had been hunted** to near extinction.*

Use: We use **past perfect passive** to talk about one event in the past that happened before another event in the past.

---

1 Read the paragraph below and underline the passive forms.

In conclusion, a number of solutions to protect endangered animals have been suggested in this essay. Previous species have been hunted and their habitats have been destroyed. However, the crucial actions of people have protected their environment and increased their numbers. Arguably, the most effective of these have been the introduction of nature reserves and prohibiting hunting. Had these solutions not been introduced, many more species would have arguably died out.

2 **Match the passive forms with their use.**

1 In conclusion, millions of hectares of habitat have been destroyed by deforestation. ___

2 Global warming has been caused by the actions of humans. ___

3 Population growth has been clearly linked to global warming. ___

a When we do not need to know who did an action or when it is already obvious who did the action

b To summarize and conclude essays and information

c When the action or the object is more important than the person who did the action

3 **Complete the passive sentences with the correct form of the verbs in the box.**

| cause   change   connect   know   show   stop |

1 CFCs _____ to be dangerous before they were banned.

2 The disposal of waste in the sea _____ to falling fish levels.

3 Before the country introduced new laws, much lost habitat _____ by deforestation.

4 The falling of the population _____ by the hunting ban.

5 In conclusion, the effects of consumer waste _____ to be the main problem affecting this country.

6 Attitudes _____ by government advertising. People now waste less water.

4 **Correct the mistakes in the sentences below. Some sentences are active.**

1 Researchers have been analyzed the cause of global warming.

2 The consequences of each solution had investigated before one was chosen.

3 The effects of rising sea levels have not yet fully understood.

4 Studies showed that 20% of the trash has been thrown from ships.

5 Environmentalists have long been campaigned for change.

5 **Use the prompts to write sentences in the passive form. Omit the original subjects if they are unnecessary.**

1 An effective way / protect / coral reefs / not / discover
   An effective way to protect coral reefs has not yet been discovered.

2 Various tactics / use / raise / the awareness of the issue

3 Researchers / growing populations of crabs / discover / in the area

4 The effects / not know / prior to the study

5 Lead in gas / prohibit / governments

6 In conclusion / the biggest damage to the ozone / cause / by CFCs

Writing skill

An essay conclusion will:

- restate the main idea in different words
- summarize the most important arguments and topics
- sometimes describe the future, such as more research that is needed or what might happen in the next few years.

Conclusions often start with phrases such as:

to conclude, in conclusion, in summary.

1 Read the conclusion. Underline the topic sentence, draw a box around the important arguments, and circle the future prediction.

To conclude, the most effective way to deal with people's carbon footprint is to provide different products and services for people. It is crucial that more renewable energy is provided to reduce the reliance on traditional fuels. Also, governments need to encourage recycling and limit the use of packaging. The future consequences of not making these changes will mean continued global warming and rising sea levels.

2 Match the topic sentences (1–3) with the sentences in the conclusions (a–c).

1 Weather-related issues are the main environmental challenge facing this country.

2 Both the government and large businesses need to work together to deal with these challenges.

3 Investment in renewable energy is one effective solution.

a Spending money on developing wind and solar power is an effective solution.

b Floods and droughts are two of the biggest issues this country currently has to deal with.

c This difficult situation can only be dealt with by cooperation between parliament and big organizations.

3 Look at the topic sentences from an essay. Paraphrase them so that you could use them in a conclusion.

1 One effective solution would be to introduce more nature reserves.

2 An immediate ban on hunting is required to save some animals from extinction.

4 Rewrite these main ideas so that you could use them to start a conclusion.

1 Recycling will play a key role in reducing the amount of waste produced by our country.

2 Unless hunting is banned, a number of animals will quickly become endangered.

Writing task

You are going to write the conclusion to an essay that answers the following question:

"Describe an environmental problem in your country and suggest ways to resolve it".

Brainstorm

Complete the brainstorm below about an environmental problem in your country and possible solutions.

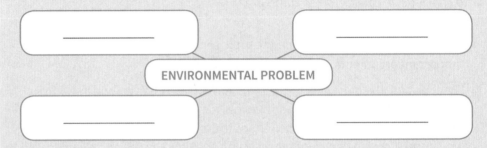

Plan

Imagine you have to write the whole essay and answer these questions.

1   What is the main problem?
2   Which is the best solution?
3   Write two arguments that explain why it is the best solution.
4   How will the solution help in the future?

Write

Use your notes from the plan to write a conclusion to the essay. Remember to use a phrase to introduce your conclusion. Pay attention to your use of present perfect passive and past perfect passive. Your text should be between 50 to 100 words long.

Share

Exchange paragraphs with a partner. Look at the checklist on page 189 and provide feedback to your partner.

Rewrite and edit

Read your partner's comments. What could you change to make your writing better? Revise your text, then check it for errors. Think about:

* the summary of your ideas
* your use of present perfect passive and past perfect passive.

Write the final draft.

Review

Wordlist

MACMILLAN
DICTIONARY

Vocabulary preview

attack (v) ***	endangered (adj)	law (n) ***	oil spill (n)
coast (n) ***	fish (v) **	livestock (n)	species (n) ***
damage (n) ***	forecast (v) *	nature reserve (n)	trade (n) ***
ecosystem (n)	hunt (v) **	ocean (n) **	tropical (adj) **

Vocabulary development

carbon footprint (n)	deforestation (n)	global warming (n) *	overfishing (n)
climate change (n)	fossil fuels (n) *	melt (v) **	overpopulation (n)

Academic words

authority (n) ***	conclusion (n) ***	crucial (adj) ***	legal (adj) ***
circumstances (n pl) ***	consequence (n) ***	disposal (n) **	prohibit (v) *

Academic words review

Complete the sentences with the words in the box.

conclusion	consequences	crucial	enables	legal

1 There are _____ for our actions and we must take responsibility for our actions.

2 The case went to court and there was a long _____ battle to establish who was at fault.

3 A passport _____ you to visit foreign countries.

4 Detective: This is a _____ piece of evidence and solves the mystery of who stole the diamond necklace. We can make an arrest!

5 Saif studied the results of his experiments carefully in order to come to a logical _____.

Unit review

Reading 1	☐ I can find phrases in a text to introduce examples.
Reading 2	☐ I can scan a text for examples in groups of three.
Study skill	☐ I can identify the correct problem-solving strategy.
Vocabulary	☐ I can use vocabulary to talk about the environment.
Grammar	☐ I can use the present and past perfect passives.
Writing	☐ I can summarize arguments to make a conclusion.

Relax AND STAY *healthy*

Discussion point

Discuss with a partner.

1 Which claims in the infographic do you think are true?

2 How do you think these ideas work?

3 What things do you do to stay healthy?

Sleep

Sleep: "stops you gaining weight," "helps to fight off illness"

Laugh

Ha Ha
Ha

Laugh: "reduces stress," "makes you feel positive"

Read

Reading: "increases intelligence," "helps you understand other people's difficulties"

VIDEO

SMART EYE EXAMS

Before you watch

Answer the questions below with a partner.

1 How many functions of a smartphone can you think of?

2 Which apps do you use? Which are most useful?

UNIT AIMS

READING 1 Making notes: using your own words
READING 2 Researching information to support your writing
STUDY SKILL Critical thinking when writing

VOCABULARY Describing symptoms
GRAMMAR Reported speech
WRITING Proofreading and editing your work

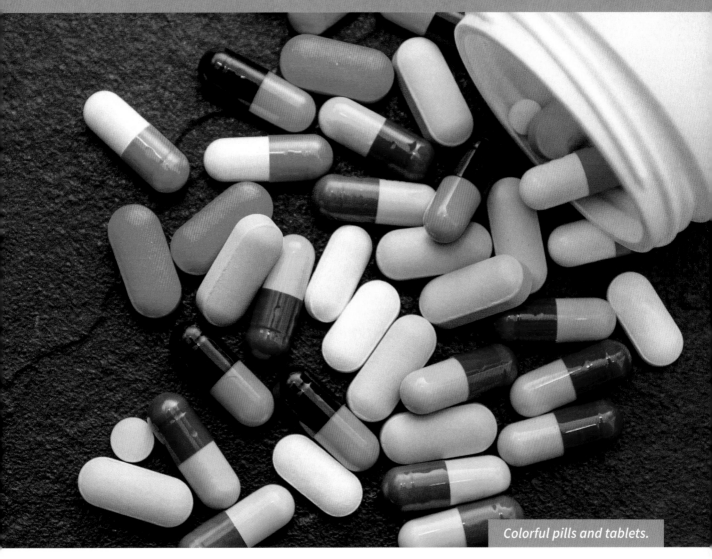

Colorful pills and tablets.

While you watch

Read the questions and then watch the video. Circle the correct answers.

1 What does the app do?

  a Records a person's location and details

  b Tells the doctor what is wrong with the eye

2 Why don't people travel to a doctor?

  a cost   b fear   c no transport

3 What percentage of people who are blind live in low-income countries?

  a 80%   b 90%   c 70%

After you watch

Answer the questions with a partner.

1 Do you ever use your phone to find out medical information?

No, because …

Yes, because …

2 What reasons do some people avoid going to the doctor for?

Some people avoid the doctor because …

3 Do you think mobile technology will become more important in medicine?

Yes, because …   *No, because …*

Self-diagnosis

A Vocabulary preview

1   Complete the sentences with the words in the box.

> allergy   condition   frightening   illness
> pharmacist   reliable   severe   wearable technology

1   I need to see the _____ this afternoon to ask about my symptoms and buy some medicine.

2   It can be _____ to read about symptoms online because it can suggest very serious illnesses.

3   You can't always trust the medical advice you get online. It's not always _____.

4   I have an _____ to fish, but my reaction is not very bad.

5   He has had a heart _____ for three years now. It affects him when he plays sports.

6   _____ now let's people check information about their health throughout the day.

7   I couldn't go to work on Monday. It wasn't serious, just a minor _____. By Tuesday it was gone.

8   My headache is so _____ I think I might have to go home.

2   Discuss these questions with a partner.

1   How often do you use a pharmacist for medical advice?

2   What medical information do you look up online?

3   Do you think that wearable technology is a reliable source of health information?

4   What is your advice for people who find doctors frightening?

B Before you read

Previewing a text

Look at the title and the glossary box. How often do you self-diagnose? What can be some of the problems of self-diagnosis?

Self-diagnosis

1   We rely on online sources for our medical problems more and more. Many people now choose to diagnose themselves online when they are sick. We are now more likely to google our symptoms before speaking to a partner, friend, family member, doctor, or pharmacist. The most common illnesses or conditions people search for are physical pains such as back pain, mental problems such as depression, food reactions such as allergies, and serious conditions such as diabetes. While many of us rely on this information, how accurate and reliable is it?

2   Many people think that the Internet has made it easier for us to diagnose our own illnesses, but research suggests that using the Internet can be a very bad way of getting the right medical treatment. The main problem comes from one of two things. Firstly, we can be too positive about how severe our symptoms are. The other problem is the opposite: some people are too negative about their situation. For example, the same symptom might be understood by one person as indigestion, but another could understand it as a heart attack.

3   These reactions and the availability of technology have led some to argue that we are creating a generation of "worried well". Sometimes people use software that is not tested or scientific to research their symptoms. In people who are already anxious, this poor information can lead to worry. Generally, the more frightening an article is, the more of your attention it is likely to get. Forums can also make people worry a lot. Anxious people are likely to then go to a doctor to find medical help even if they don't always need it. The main problem actually comes from people who do not worry as much though. If they do not diagnose themselves accurately, they may not go to a doctor even though they have a serious medical condition.

4   A new kind of online software is called a symptom checker. These programs try to analyze our symptoms and offer advice as to whether we should seek further medical help, such as go to see a doctor or pharmacist. Researchers at the Harvard Medical School found that, although these programs are often wrong, they are more accurate than a general Internet search. However, getting the right diagnosis might not be as important as getting the right advice about whether, or how quickly, to visit a doctor. Under tests, for symptoms that were severe and would need emergency care, the researchers found that the software was right 80% of the time, but Internet searches for the same information were only right 64% of the time.

5   At the moment, self-diagnosis is quite basic, but some argue that we will have much more sophisticated self-care in place in the next 20 years. For example, body scanners in shops might be able to diagnose illnesses faster and more effectively than doctors. The system could also give drugs, like a pharmacist does, and make appointments with a doctor. This, along with using wearable technology such as watches, means we could have dozens of daily statistics about our health. In just a few years, googling your symptoms could seem quite an old-fashioned method as technology starts to constantly check our health.

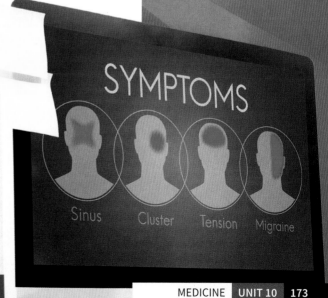

GLOSSARY
diagnose (v) to find out what physical or mental problem someone has by examining them
diagnosis (n) a statement about what disease someone has, based on examining them
indigestion (n) feeling unwell from eating food, often too quickly

Taking notes: using your
own words

C Global reading

We often take notes when we read to help research a topic or prepare for an essay. Taking notes in your own words is important. It will help you avoid potential plagiarism (copying other people's work). Writing notes in your own words also helps you understand what you are reading and writing about, rather than just copying what you read.

Higher numbers of people use the Internet when they are ill. It is also
the most popular source. People look for a wide range of health issues
including major illnesses.

1 Match words and phrases in the notes with the things they paraphrase in the text.

    1 ill _____

    2 source _____

    3 health issues _____

    4 major illnesses _____

2 Make notes in your own words on these topics.

    1 Two main problems with diagnosing ourselves

    2 The effects of worrying

    3 Symptom checkers

    4 Self-diagnosis and technology in the future

D Close reading

Scanning

Read the text. Write *T* (True), *F* (False), or *NG* (Not Given) for each sentence.

1 People often check physical symptoms, like back pain, online. ___

2 The Internet makes everyone worry about their health more. ___

3 The accuracy of medical information on the Internet has improved. ___

4 We pay more attention to articles that make us worry. ___

5 Symptom checkers are better than the Internet in general. ___

6 Doctors will work largely online with patients in the future. ___

E Critical thinking

1 When do you think self-diagnosis is positive? Can you give an example?

2 What are some of the dangers of self-diagnosis? What makes you say that?

Study skills | Critical thinking when writing

Use evidence to support your reasoning

A large part of any assignment will consist of deciding on and presenting the best evidence to support your argument.

Take multiple perspectives

The best answers identify how and why various experts agree or disagree on an issue, and demonstrate how the evidence supports, or does not support, their positions.

Analyze your own work critically

Your tutors or examiners will take a critical approach when marking your work. Before handing in an assignment, analyze it critically, as you would other material you read.

© Stella Cottrell (2013)

1   Discuss with a partner. When you find a source, how do you decide whether it is a good source to use in your essay? Think about:

accuracy   date   relevance to the topic   the author   the reason it was written

2   Read *Critical thinking when writing* and then discuss these questions with a partner.

1   How can you decide whether an expert wrote the text?

2   Some writers want to present particular arguments. How can you make sure your essay will be balanced?

3   How do you decide whether a website is reliable or not?

3   Look at these comments from teachers. What does each person need to do to improve their writing?

1   More critical analysis needed.

   This person needs to not just repeat information from sources. They need to give their opinion. They need to look at the strengths and weaknesses.

2   You have only described the theory. You need to evaluate it.

3   Your essay is based only on personal opinion.

4   Think about the last feedback you received. Write a checklist for the areas you need to improve.

A good night's sleep

A Vocabulary preview

1 Match the words in bold with the correct definitions.

1	**exercise** (n)	a	the process of becoming heavier
2	**mental health** (n)	b	the standard to which someone does something such as a job or an examination
3	**performance** (n)		
4	**physically** (adv)	c	working hard and producing or achieving a lot
5	**productive** (adj)	d	in an important way
6	**regularly** (adv)	e	the condition of your mind
7	**significantly** (adv)	f	in a way that is related to your body or appearance
8	**weight gain** (n)		
		g	often
		h	physical activity done in order to stay healthy and make your body stronger

2 Complete the sentences with words from Exercise 1.

1 I am more _____ and achieve a lot more when I sleep well.

2 I _____ get less than six hours' sleep a night.

3 My _____ improves with good sleep. I feel calmer, more relaxed, and less stressed.

4 When I work hard _____, for example in the garden, I sleep a lot better.

5 I eat a lot of sugary foods to stay awake. Unfortunately, this leads to _____.

6 When I do _____ I get better sleep. Especially when it is outside.

7 My _____ at work is much worse when I don't get a good night's sleep. The standard improves with sleep.

8 When I don't sleep well for a week it _____ impacts on my health.

3 Check (✓) the sentences that you agree with in Exercise 2. Compare your choices with a partner.

B Before you read

Preparing to read

Think of three ways a lack of sleep can affect your health. Compare your ideas with a partner.

A good night's *sleep*

GLOSSARY

immune system (n) the body's way of dealing with illnesses and keeping us healthy

obese (adj) too fat, in a way that is dangerous for your health

type 2 diabetes (n) when your body does not produce enough of the hormone insulin. This type of diabetes is usually caused by lifestyle

1 Many people enjoy a good night's sleep, but we often feel guilty for spending too much time in bed. However, a good night's sleep is just as important for our health as a good diet and exercising. Unfortunately, modern complex lives are making it harder and harder to sleep at normal times and to sleep well. So what effect does a poor night's sleep have on our bodies?

2 One of the biggest negative health effects is that people who do not sleep well are likely to gain weight. It is in fact one of the biggest causes of obesity. People who sleep for a short amount of time have between a 55% and 89% chance of becoming obese. This occurs largely because people who sleep less tend to eat more because they feel tired and need more energy. They also eat more of the wrong things. When we do not get enough sleep, our bodies produce higher levels of the hormone ghrelin which makes us eat more. To gain more energy quickly we also tend to seek out comfort foods that are high in fat and sugar. At the same time, we do not have enough of the hormone leptin. This hormone does the opposite—it tells us when to stop eating. These hormone changes dramatically affect the way we consume food.

3 In addition to weight gain, poor sleepers are also at a much higher risk of various other serious illnesses and diseases. Firstly, people who sleep less than seven to eight hours per night have an increased risk of a heart attack or stroke. It also significantly increases the risk of type 2 diabetes. In one study, reducing sleep to four hours per night for just six nights led to the people developing pre-diabetes symptoms. Sleep is also important for boosting our immune system and helps in the process of recovery from minor illnesses. People who sleep less than seven hours a night are much more likely to develop a cold than those who sleep eight or more hours a night.

4 As well as affecting people physically, extreme tiredness, or fatigue, can have severe negative mental effects. Bad sleep, tiredness, and fatigue also cause, and can be a symptom of, depression. Our mental health also depends on our social groups and interacting with other people. Unfortunately, if we do not get enough sleep, we are not able to interact as well with others. We cannot read other people's emotions well when we are tired so we cannot recognize when people are angry or happy. In other words, we cannot judge how people feel and how we should react.

5 All of these effects show how sleep, or lack of sleep, can change individual people's lives. However, they also can have an impact on society as a whole. When it comes to work and education, our ability to concentrate, focus on work, and be precise can depend on how well we've slept. How much we achieve is also reduced when we do not get enough sleep. We are much more likely to make a mistake at work or during school when we have poor-quality sleep. While this might not matter in some roles, for those who can put others in danger of injury or even death, such as doctors, drivers of vehicles, and operators of machines, it can make a big difference. Good sleep, on the other hand, can increase our ability to solve problems and improve our memory performance.

6 So, what can be done to help improve the quality of sleep across society? One important issue is to consider the circadian rhythm of the body. The circadian rhythm is our natural sleep pattern, in other words, the natural time our bodies want to go to sleep. This varies from person to person to some extent but the biggest differences are between different generations. Firstly, young babies need *significantly* more sleep than adults, and teenagers need *slightly* more sleep than adults. However, even more importantly, because of the hormones released in our body, these different age groups need to sleep at different times. For example, a ten-year-old child cannot focus on academic work before 8:30 in the morning whereas a teenager or college student cannot really work well before 10 a.m. Studies in the U.K. have shown that when schools change the hours pupils start school, there is a significant improvement in academic performance. Even with adults, the normal nine-to-five routine of work does not match our body clock (circadian rhythm) until we reach the age of 55.

7 Arguably, the health of societies across the world is suffering because we do not get enough sleep and we are not allowed to sleep and work at the right times. Working shifts can significantly increase your risk of heart disease, cancer, and diabetes. It can make your life shorter. While not quite so severe, even just working or studying during the "wrong" hours can affect people's health and performance. Simply changing the start and finish time of school and work could improve the health of whole generations. Academic performance would improve and employees would be happier and more productive. One factor that wins many arguments is money—what is something worth? Arguably, the countries and companies that are willing to change their working day to improve the health of employees could ultimately become the richest and most successful as they have the most productive staff.

C Global reading

Read *A good night's sleep* and complete the summary.

People who do not sleep well tend to eat more of the wrong foods. This is because the body produces more ¹_____ which leads to people consuming more. We also produce less ²_____ which tells us when we have eaten enough. People who do not sleep enough also have more chance of getting an ³_____. When we don't get enough sleep, we can become depressed and we can't ⁴_____ as well with others. Our ability to perform tasks is also reduced. In some jobs this may cause an ⁵_____ or even result in people dying. The ⁶_____ is the body's natural clock and this changes over different ages. Starting work at nine and finishing at five only works for people aged ⁷_____.

D Close reading

When you write an academic essay, you will need to do research and read articles to find information that supports your ideas. Make notes before you read on questions or ideas you have. Then as you read, record any information you find that does or doesn't support these ideas.

Read the text and underline support for these ideas.

1 People who lack sleep may gain weight.

2 Our bodies want to eat the wrong foods when we are tired.

3 Poor sleep could lead to serious medical conditions.

4 Poor sleep can affect our mental health.

5 People of different ages need different amounts of sleep.

6 People should not start school or college early.

E Critical thinking

1 What do you think would be the main benefit of better sleep for you?

I think the main benefit would be …

2 Do you think it would be a good idea to change the hours of school and work? Why?

I do / don't think it would be a good idea because …

Vocabulary development

Words to describe medical symptoms

1 Match the words in bold with the correct definitions.

1	**ache** (n)	a	painful and uncomfortable, usually as a result of an injury, infection, or too much exercise
2	**cough** (v)	b	to force air up through your throat with a sudden noise, especially when you have a cold
3	**dizzy** (adj)		
4	**fever** (n)	c	happening or done now, without any delay
5	**immediate** (adj)	d	needing immediate attention
6	**sore** (adj)	e	not having much strength or energy
7	**urgent** (adj)	f	a continuous pain but not a strong pain
8	**weak** (adj)	g	feeling as if you or the things around you are spinning, especially when you think you are going to fall
		h	a medical condition in which the temperature of your body is very high and you feel ill

2 Complete the sentences with words from Exercise 1.

1 My legs are _____ after going for a run yesterday.

2 I have a _____. My temperature is really high.

3 My throat is really sore from my bad _____.

4 I think I stood up too quickly. I feel _____.

5 I feel really _____. I don't have the energy to get out of bed.

6 The pain isn't strong but it's a constant _____.

7 I think you need _____ medical help. That does not look good.

8 You should only go to a hospital for _____ problems.

3 Discuss these questions with a partner.

1 How important is healthy living to you?

2 How do you feel when you don't sleep or eat well?

3 Are the physical or mental effects of poor sleep worse?

Academic words

1 Match the words in bold with the correct definitions.

1 **concentrate** (v)
2 **consume** (v)
3 **injury** (n)
4 **interact** (v)
5 **minor** (adj)
6 **precise** (adj)
7 **process** (n)
8 **recovery** (n)

a physical damage done to a person or a part of their body

b to communicate with and react to another person

c not very important in comparison with people or things of the same type

d to eat or drink something

e exact and accurate

f a series of things that happen and have a particular result

g becoming fit and healthy again

h to give all your attention to the thing you are doing

2 Complete the sentences with words from Exercise 1.

1 I'm trying to _____ less sugar.

2 He has broken his leg. It's a serious _____.

3 I can _____ on my work better when I drink a lot of water.

4 It's only a _____ injury. I don't think I need to go to the doctor.

5 It's important to use a _____ amount of medicine. Too much is dangerous.

6 I feel depressed when I don't _____ with other people for a few days.

7 There are four stages in the _____.

8 It takes about three weeks to get better and make a full _____.

3 Discuss these questions with a partner.

1 What injuries have you had in your life? Which had the hardest recovery?

2 Do you agree that both physical and mental strength are important if you want to succeed?

3 What helps you to concentrate better?

Writing model

You are going to learn about reported speech and about proofreading your writing. You are then going to write and edit an essay to answer a question about diagnosing and treating yourself at home.

A Analyze

Which ideas from the box below are mentioned in the model answer? Read the text. Underline the relevant fragments.

Agree	Disagree
Quick diagnosis	Mistakes can be made
Saves money	Problem in serious illnesses
Takes pressure off doctors	Doctors do not write the information
More effective	

B Model

There is a large amount of information available online to help people check their symptoms and diagnose themselves when they are ill. While this information is useful, this essay will argue that people should not rely on the information because it is not precise enough.

Studies have found that more and more people believe the Internet is a useful source of medical information. They can enter symptoms, such as weak or dizzy, into software or a search engine and use the results to try to diagnose their illness or injury quickly. This process can stop people going to the doctors when it is not necessary and take pressure off doctors and hospitals.

However, a lot of the information is inaccurate and people can often make mistakes when trying to diagnose or treat themselves. A recent study found that one person may enter the same symptoms as another and reach a completely different conclusion. While this does not matter for minor illnesses it presents big risks in the case of an emergency.

In conclusion, while the Internet may be a useful and a growing source of medical information, people do not have the knowledge and skills to diagnose themselves. As a result, people should not rely on the Internet to decide what illness they have or they could delay their recovery.

1 Read the model answer and answer the questions.

   1 Which sentence in the introduction gives the main opinion?

   2 In the main body, does the writer present their view or the other arguments first?

   3 Which sentence in the conclusion paraphrases the main argument?

2 Work with a partner. When would you look up symptoms online?

Grammar

Reported speech

We use reported speech when we want to report what someone else has said. In academic writing this is often used when directly or indirectly quoting research or another text.

When reporting we often change the tense, e.g.

Simple present > simple past

Direct speech: *"Our research shows that more people use the Internet for self-diagnosis," reported the doctor.*

Reported speech: *The doctor reported that the research showed more people used the Internet for self-diagnosis.*

Other tense changes include:
Present perfect > past perfect   simple past > past perfect   will > would

We also change the pronoun when we use reported speech:

Mike said, "I feel ill."

Mike said that he felt ill.

It is also important to use a range of specific verbs in academic written work, e.g.

She had claimed … Scientists would argue …

1   Rewrite the sentences in reported speech.

1   The researchers said, "The Internet is not very accurate for medical diagnosis."

_____

2   The doctor said, "I have had a big increase in patients self-diagnosing."

_____

3   A leading psychologist said, "The participants showed increased levels of depression when they had under six hours' sleep for more than a week."

_____

4   One scientist said, "Society will develop further health problems because of poor sleep."

_____

5   The lecturer suggested, "You need to do the test on more people."

_____

2 Match the reporting verb with its meaning.

1 **argue**   a to give details about what someone or something is like

2 **claim**   b to say that something is true, even if there is no definite proof

3 **describe**

4 **prove**   c to give reasons why you believe that something is right or true

5 **report**   d to say something clearly

6 **state**   e to provide evidence that shows that something is true

f to provide information about something that exists or has happened

3 **Write these sentences in reported speech using the verbs in parentheses.**

1 Peterson: "Starting work at nine is not effective." (claim)
   Peterson claimed that starting work at nine was not effective.

2 Leading doctors: "People need eight hours' sleep to have a healthy body." (state)

   _____

3 Analysts: "Internet diagnosis will be more accurate in the future." (report)

   _____

4 Smith: "Self-diagnosis can increase levels of stress and anxiety." (describe)

   _____

5 University researchers: "The technology has not been 100% accurate." (argue)

   _____

6 Academics: "Concentration levels fall dramatically with only six hours' sleep." (prove)

   _____

Writing skill

Before handing in your work it is important to check your work for grammar errors, spelling, punctuation, structure, and academic style. Each one should be checked in a separate stage and not at the same time.

1 Correct the mistakes in these sentences.

1 More and more patients is diagnosing themselves online.

2 If people will diagnose themselves online, they won't do so accurately.

3 The Internet has became a valuable source of information.

4 People with the same symptoms do not always think the same illness.

5 Recent studies had shown that self-diagnosis on the Internet is not very accurate.

2 Which word is spelled correctly in each group?

1	compltly	environmental	localy
2	achieve	respons	contrebution
3	demonstrat	comunity	maintenance
4	minimzed	philosofy	consequence

3 Correct the incorrect spellings in Exercise 2.

4 Look at the introduction to the essay question. What is missing from the introduction?

"We should diagnose and treat ourselves at home before going to the doctor. To what extent do you agree or disagree?"

More and more people are using the Internet and other programs to diagnose themselves at home. Self-diagnosis can save time, but many of the programs are not very accurate.

Writing task

Write an opinion essay to answer the question:
"We should diagnose and treat ourselves at home before going to the doctor.
To what extent do you agree or disagree?"

Brainstorm

Look back at your notes on *Self diagnosis*. Use the notes to help you brainstorm the advantages and disadvantages of treating and diagnosing ourselves.

Reasons to agree	Reasons to disagree

Plan

1 Choose two reasons to agree and two reasons to disagree to focus on.

2 Decide whether you think the reasons to agree or disagree are stronger.

3 Summarize your main opinion in one sentence.

Write

Using your brainstorm and plan write your essay. Pay attention to your reported speech. Proofread your work for errors with grammar, spelling, and punctuation. Your essay should be 200 to 250 words long.

Share

Exchange essay with a partner. Look at the checklist on page 189 and provide feedback to your partner.

Rewrite and edit

Read your partner's comments. What could you change to make your writing better? Revise your text, then check it for errors. Think about:

• your use of reported speech

• errors you usually make (check these carefully).

Write the final draft.

Review

Wordlist

MACMILLAN DICTIONARY

Vocabulary preview

allergy (n)	illness (n) ***	physically (adv) **	severe (adj) ***
condition (n) ***	mental health (n)	productive (adj) **	significantly (adv) **
exercise (n) ***	performance (n) ***	regularly (adv) ***	wearable technology (n)
frightening (adj) *	pharmacist (n)	reliable (adj) **	weight gain (n)

Vocabulary development

ache (n) *	dizzy (adj)	immediate (adj) ***	urgent (adj) **
cough (v) *	fever (n) *	sore (adj) *	weak (adj) ***

Academic words

concentrate (v) ***	injury (n) ***	minor (adj) ***	process (n) ***
consume (v) **	interact (v) *	precise (adj) **	recovery (n) ***

Academic words review

Complete the sentences with the words in the box.

authority	consume	injury	interact	recovery

1 Did you know that African elephants _____ up to 250 kilograms of food per day? How about that!

2 It is so interesting to people-watch and see how they _____ with one another.

3 The economy is getting better, but it is going to be a slow _____.

4 The higher your position in a company, the more _____ you have.

5 You must wear protective gear in the factory to avoid _____.

Unit review

Reading 1 ☐ I can make notes using my own words.

Reading 2 ☐ I can research for information to support my writing.

Study skill ☐ I can think critically when writing.

Vocabulary ☐ I can describe the symptoms of common illnesses.

Grammar ☐ I can use reported speech.

Writing ☐ I can proofread and edit my work.

Functional language phrase bank

The phrases below give common ways of expressing useful functions.
Use them to help you as you're completing the *Discussion point* and *Critical thinking* activities.

Asking for clarification
Sorry, can you explain that some more?
Could you say that another way?
When you say … do you mean …?
Sorry, I don't follow that.
What do you mean?

Asking for repetition
Could you repeat that, please?
I'm sorry, I didn't catch that.
Could you say that again?

When you don't know the word for something
What does … mean?
Sorry, I'm not sure what … means.

Working with a partner
Would you like to start?
Shall I go first?
Shall we do this one first?
Where do you want to begin?

Giving opinions
I think that …
It seems to me that …
In my opinion …
As I see it …

Agreeing and disagreeing
I know what you mean.
That's true.
You have a point there.
Yes. I see what you're saying, but …
I understand your point, but …
I don't think that's true.

Asking for opinions
Do you think …?
Do you feel …?

What do you think about …?
How about you, Jennifer? What do you think?
What about you?
Does anyone have any other ideas?
Do you have any thoughts on this?

Asking for more information
In what way?
Why do you think that?
Can you give an example?

Not giving a strong preference
It doesn't matter to me.
I don't really have a strong preference.
I've never really thought about that.
Either is fine.

Expressing interest
I'd like to hear more about that.
That sounds interesting.
How interesting!
Tell me more about that.

Giving reasons
This is … because …
This has to be … because …
I think … because …

Checking understanding
Do you know what I mean?
Do you see what I'm saying?
Are you following me?

Putting things in order
This needs to come first because …
I think this is the most / least important because …
For me, this is the most / least relevant because …

Writing task peer review checklist

Use the checklist below as you read over your partner's work.

1 Does the paragraph / essay have these things:

   name
   class
   the date
   a title

2 Does the paragraph or essay introduction directly answer the writing assignment?

3 Does every sentence begin and end with correct punctuation?

4 What is your favorite sentence or point from the paragraph?

5 Did you notice any target vocabulary from the unit? Write it here:

6 Highlight any target grammar from the unit.

7 Underline the topic sentence or sentences.

8 Write one question about the paragraph / essay for the writer.

Academic words revision

Units 1–5

Complete the sentences with the words in the box.

community consumer contribution
features maintain network target trend

1 One of the most striking _____ of Dubai is how clean it is.

2 Sales are good this month. We are expecting to reach our _____.

3 There are some strong personalities in our class and it is difficult for everyone to _____ good relationships.

4 People need to feel that they belong somewhere. They need to feel that they are part of a _____.

5 LinkedIn is an excellent way of developing a _____ of contacts who have the same interests as you.

6 _____ goods are the things you buy for yourself and for your home, such as clothing and furniture.

7 Professor Stephen Hawking has made an enormous _____ to our understanding of the universe.

8 When an item, such as a piece of clothing or a gadget is very fashionable we say it is "on _____."

Units 6–10

Complete the sentences with the words in the box.

aware confirmed disposal external focus locate prohibited revolution

1 Final examinations are usually marked by an _____ examiner—not someone from the university.

2 We looked carefully at the map, but we couldn't _____ the hotel we were planning to stay in. It wasn't on the map.

3 You are not allowed to take guns or knives onto the aircraft. They are _____ items.

4 The Industrial _____ was the time when Britain's economy changed from being agricultural to being industrial.

5 We are going to Florida on vacation! Our flights and hotel reservations have been _____.

6 Thank you for reporting this problem. I wasn't _____ of it before.

7 Waste _____ is a real problem for many countries—where and how to get rid of our trash.

8 In my presentation today, I will _____ on three main topics.

Macmillan Education
4 Crinan Street
London N1 9XW
A division of Macmillan Publishers Limited
Companies and representatives throughout the world

ISBN 978-1-380-00528-1

Written by Louis Rogers
Series Consultant Dorothy E. Zemach

The author has asserted his right to be identified as the author of this work in accordance with the Copyright, Designs and Patents Act 1988.

This edition published 2018

First edition entitled "Skillful" published 2012 by Macmillan Publishers Limited

Designed by emc design ltd
Illustrated by emc design ltd and Carl Morris (Beehive Illustration) pp 92, 96
Cover design by emc design ltd
Cover picture by Sam Parij (Eye Candy Illustration)/Getty Images/ Moment Open/Alicia Llop
Picture research by Emily Taylor

The publishers would like to thank the following for their thoughtful insights and perceptive comments during the development of the material:

Dalal Al Hitty, University of Bahrain, Bahrain; Karin Heuert Galvão, i-Study Interactive Learning, São Paulo, Brazil; Ohanes Sakris, Australian College of Kuwait, Kuwait; Eoin Jordan, Xi'an Jiaotong-Liverpool University, Suzhou, China; Aaron Rotsinger, Xi'an Jiaotong-Liverpool University, Suzhou, China; Dr. Osman Z. Barnawi, Royal Commission Yanbu Colleges & Institutes, Yanbu, Saudi Arabia; Andrew Lasher, SUNY Korea, Incheon, South Korea; Fatoş Uğur Eskiçırak, Bahçeşehir University, Istanbul, Turkey; Dr. Asmaa Awad, University of Sharjah, Sharjah, United Arab Emirates; Amy Holtby, The Petroleum Institute, Abu Dhabi, United Arab Emirates; Dr. Christina Gitsaki, Zayed University, Dubai, United Arab Emirates.

The authors and publishers would like to thank the following for permission to reproduce their images:

Alamy/Classic Image p137(br), Alamy/Flowerphotos p39, Alamy/GL Archive p137(tr), Alamy/OJO Images Ltd p177, Alamy/Rawpixel Ltd p173, Alamy/SFM Stock 4 p134-135, Alamy/Stacy Walsh Rosenstock p87(tr) **Brand X** p33(t); **Getty Images**/AFP/Adrian Dennis p62-63, Getty Images/ AFP/Greg Wood p98-99, Getty Images/Emmanuel Aguirre p119, Getty Images/Theo Allofs p158, Getty Images/Andrearoad p29, Getty Images/ AWL Images p123, Getty Images/Scott Barbour p116-117, Getty Images/ Blend Images p106, Getty Images/Brand New Images p111, Getty Images/ Cultura Exclusive p83, Getty Images/Georgette Douwma pp155, 156, Getty Images/Feng Wei Photography p159,, Getty Images/Patrick Foto p80-81, Getty Images/Michael Haegele p146, Getty Images/Image Source p15, Getty Images/iStockphoto p33(b), , Getty Images/iStockPhoto/Apbalboa p57, Getty Images/iStockphoto/Cyano66 p139, Getty Images/iStockPhoto/ Emesilva p34, Getty Images/iStockphoto/JK1991 p170-171, Getty Images/ iStockPhoto/Courtney Keating p56, Getty Images/iStockphoto/Correia Patrice p160, Getty Images/iStockphoto/Yobro10 p101, Getty Images/ Laflor p47, Getty Images/Lonely Planet Images/Michael Marquand p88, Getty Images/Maica p142(br), Getty Images/Paul McGee p118, Getty Images/Bruno Morandi p26-27, Getty Images/Kelvin Murray p11, Getty Images/National Geographic Magazines p162, Getty Images/Oxford Scientific RM p124, Getty Images/Andrew Rich p105, Getty Images/Henrik Sorensen p14, Getty Images/StockstudioX p8-9, Getty Images/Claire Takacs p87(b), Getty Images/Ramin Talaie p51; **PlainPicture**/Westend61/ Hans Clausen p152-153, PlainPicture/Westend61/Zerocreatives p65; **Rex Features**/Chameleons Eye/Shutterstock p36, Rex Features/Connection/ Shutterstock p141, Rex Features/Newscast/Shutterstock p142(bl), Rex Features/Nico Hermann/Shutterstock p180, Rex Features/Robertharding/ Shutterstock p137(background); **SuperStock**/Suedhang p44-45; Thomson Reuters pp8, 26, 44, 62, 80, 98, 116, 134-135, 152, 170.

Printed and bound in Dubai
2022 2021 2020 2019 2018
10 9 8 7 6 5 4 3 2 1

PALGRAVE STUDY SKILLS

by bestselling author, **Stella Cottrell**

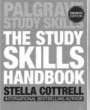

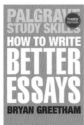

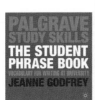
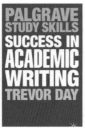

palgravestudyskills.com

f facebook.com/skills4study

𝕏 twitter.com/skills4study